ATHEISM

by

Joseph Lewis

Author of "The Tyranny of God," "The Bible Unmasked,"
"Lincoln, the Freethinker," "Burbank, the Infidel," "Jefferson, the Freethinker," "Franklin, the Freethinker," "Voltaire, the Incomparable Infidel," "The Bible and the Public Schools," "Shall Children Receive Religious Instruction?"
"Mexico and the Church," "Spain: Land Blighted by Religion," etc.

THE FREETHOUGHT PRESS ASSOCIATION, INC.

317 EAST 34th STREET, NEW YORK, N. Y.

THE COMMUNITY CHURCH
PARK AVENUE AND THIRTY-FOURTH STREET
NEW YORK CITY

April 21, 1930

Dear Mr. Lewis:

I want to thank you this morning
for the great service which you did us last night.
Your address was brilliant in the extreme, altogether the best statement I have every heard on the
question of atheism.   I feel deeply grateful to
you for this carefully prepared contribution to the
evening's discussion.

Very sincerely yours,

John Haynes Holmes

This address on Atheism was delivered at a Symposium on "Present Religious Tendencies", held at the Community Church, 34th Street and Park Avenue, New York City, on the Evening of April 20th, 1930. The other speakers were Mr. Stanley High, Editor of the Christian Herald, and Reverend Charles Francis Potter, Minister, First Humanist Society of New York. Reverend John Haynes Holmes, minister of the Community Church, was Chairman.

"Is it to the interest of a man to be a boy all his life?"

THOMAS PAINE

Both of my colleagues on this platform have been especially trained to espouse the cause they have presented tonight.

Both were trained to be ministers of religion.

And although only one of them still occupies the pulpit, the other is the editor of a religious magazine.

Both have faithfully fulfilled their training. And it would be unusual if that were not the case.

We cannot expect a man trained to be a carpenter to be able to carve statues like a Rodin. We cannot expect a man trained to be a bricklayer to be able to paint pictures like a Rembrandt.

If by some chance we find one who possesses a natural talent, and is able to rise above the level of his training, that exception only proves the rule.

I was never trained to espouse the cause of Atheism.

I came to accept Atheism as the result of independent thought and self-study. And although as a child I was instructed in the religion of my parents, I never came under the spell of religious training long enough to so warp my mentality as not to be able to see any other viewpoint.

I came to my conclusions after a full analysis and an impartial consideration of the various religious creeds and the different systems of philosophy.

In my study of the different fields of thought, I found no philosophy that contained so many truths, and inspired one with so much courage, as Atheism.

Atheism equips us to face life, with its multitude of trials and tribulations, better than any other code of living that I have yet been able to find.

It is grounded in the very roots of life itself.

Its foundation is based upon Nature, without superfluities and false garments.

It stands unadorned, requiring nothing but its own nudity to give it strength, and charm and beauty.

No sham or shambles are attached to it.

Atheism Rises Above Creeds

Atheism rises above creeds and puts Humanity upon one plane.

There can be no "chosen people" in the Atheist philosophy.

There are no bended knees in Atheism;

No supplications, no prayers;

No sacrificial redemptions;

No "divine" revelations;

No washing in the blood of the lamb;

No crusades, no massacres, no holy wars;

No heaven, no hell, no purgatory;

No silly rewards and no vindictive punishments;

No christs, and no saviors;

No devils, no ghosts and no gods.

Atheism breaks down the barriers of nationalities and like "one touch of nature makes the whole world kin."

Systems of religion make people clannish and bigoted.

Their chief aim and interest in life is to gather together and pick out the faults of others and reveal their secret hatred of those who do not believe as they do.

Atheism Is Mental Freedom

Atheism is a vigorous and a courageous philosophy.

It is not afraid to face the problems of life, and it is not afraid to confess that there are problems yet to be solved.

It does not claim that it has solved all the questions of the universe, but it does claim that it has discovered the approach and learned the method of solving them.

It has dedicated itself to a passionate quest for the truth.

It believes that truth for truth's sake is the highest ideal. And that virtue is its own reward.

It believes that love of humanity is a higher ideal than a love of God. We cannot help God, but we can help mankind. "Hands that help are better far than lips that play." Praying to God is humiliating; worshipping God degrading.

It believes with Ingersoll, when he said: "Give me the storm and tempest of thought and action rather than the dead calm of ignorance and faith. Banish me from Eden when you will, but first let me eat of the fruit of the tree of knowledge."

Atheism is a self-reliant philosophy.

It makes a man intellectually free. He is thrilled to enthusiasm by his mental emancipation and he faces the universe without fear of ghosts or gods.

It teaches man that unless he devotes his energies and applies himself whole-heartedly to the task he wishes to achieve, the accomplishment will not be made.

It warns him that any reliance upon prayers or "divine" help will prove a bitter disappointment.

To the philosophy of Atheism belongs the credit of robbing Death of its horror and its terror.

If Atheism writes upon the blackboard of the Universe a question mark, it writes it for the purpose of stating that there is a question yet to be answered.

Is it not better to place a question mark upon a problem while seeking an answer than to put the label "God" there and consider the matter solved?

THE ASYLUM OF IGNORANCE

Does not the word "God" only confuse and make more difficult the solution by assuming a conclusion that is utterly groundless and palpably absurd?

"God," said Spinoza, "is the Asylum of Ignorance."

No better description has ever been uttered.

Shelley said God was a hypothesis, and, as such, required proof. Can any minister of any denomination of any religion supply that proof?

Facts and not merely opinions are what we want. Emotionalism is not a substitute for the truth.

If Atheism is sometimes called a "negative" philosophy, it is because the conditions of life make a negative philosophy best suited to meet the exigencies of existence, and only in that sense can it be called negative.

Some ministers of religion ignorantly call Atheism a negative philosophy because Atheism must first destroy the monumental ignorance and the degrading superstition with which religion, throughout the ages, has so shamelessly stultified the brain of man.

A negative attitude in life is sometimes essential to proper conduct.

Life itself very often depends upon negation.

It is a negative attitude when we are cautious about over-eating. It is a negative attitude when we do not indulge our appetites, or give vent to our impulses.

And on many occasions I have seen illustrated editorials sermonizing upon the fact that the hardest word in our language to pronounce is the word "NO!"

It is only when we have the courage to say NO to certain temptations that we can avoid the consequences that are the results of following those temptations.

Progress also very often consists in negation.

Man finds himself in a universe utterly unprepared and poorly equipped to face the facts and conditions of life.

He must overcome the illusions and the deceptive forces that are forever present in Nature.

When the light of intelligence first came into the mentality of man, he found himself in a world that was a wilderness; a world reeking with pestilence and populated with shrieking beasts and brutal and savage people.

No wonder that Man's distorted intellect gave rise to a series of ideas concerning God that makes one shudder at their hideousness.

His primitive imagination conceived gods of a multitude of heads, of grotesque parts, of several bodies, of numberless eyes and legs and arms.

In order that man may think clearly and rationally upon the facts of life, all these concepts must be destroyed.

That is only one of the tasks of Atheism.

"To free a man from error is to give, not take away," said Schopenhauer.

NEW GODS—WHAT FOR?

Some of our present-day humanists, emancipated to the degree that they no longer accept deities like "Jehovah," cry for a new concept of God. They want something to put in the place of what has been taken away.

Do they want also a substitute for Hell?

And what would be their answer to this question, "If the Devil should die would God make another?"

They are like children crying for the moon.

Will anyone be so good as to tell me what we need a new concept of God for? Haven't we had gods enough? Hasn't it been task enough to get rid of the conglomeration that has already plagued the human race?

I plead that we no longer contaminate heaven with these

hideous creatures and frightful monsters of religious hallucinations.

DESTRUCTIVE OF SUPERSTITION

Ministers also take delight in saying that Atheism is dogmatic and destructive.

If Atheism is called dogmatic it is because dogmatism is the
law of nature.

A fact is the most stubborn thing in the world. Matter in-
sits upon occupying space all by itself and motion will continue in motion regardless of the opinions concerning it.

Time does not stop to listen to prayers.

> "The Moving Finger writes; and having writ,
>   Moves on; nor all your Piety nor Wit
> Shall lure it back to cancel half a line,
>   Nor all your tears wash out a word of it."

And Atheism is destructive in the same sense that Columbus was a destroyer, when he corrected the erroneous conception, induced by false theological ideas, of the flatness of the
earth, when he sailed across the ocean and proved the rotun-
dity of the planet upon which we live.

Atheism is destructive in the same sense that Galileo was a
destroyer, when he corrected the erroneous conception, induced by false theological ideas, concerning the existence of
only one moon, when he discovered the satellites of Jupiter.

And so throughout the history of intellectual progress is
this attitude true. Call it negative, call it dogmatic, call it
destructive, call it what you will. It is the main spring of
progress.

Is a physician destructive when he cures a patient of disease?

A CURE FOR MENTAL DISORDER

The human race has suffered for centuries and is still suffering from the mental disorder known as religion, and Atheism
is the only physician that will be able to effect a permanent
cure.

No wonder the great Buckle was prompted to say:

"Every great reform which has been effected has consisted,
not in doing something new, but in undoing something old."

But what hypocrisy it is on the part of ministers of religion
to call Atheism a negative philosophy, when their own Ten
Commandments are a series of "Thou shalt nots"—

But Atheism is also an aggressive and a militant and a constructive philosophy.

It is interested in the HERE and NOW.

It finds problems enough here that require immediate solution and does not fly to others that it knows not of.

Man Must Help Himself

Atheism cannot sit idly by and watch injustice perpetrated, nor permit the exploitation of the weak by the strong.

Its ideal is the establishment of justice—man-made justice, even though it be.

If man waited for God to feed him he would starve to death.

Atheism believes in education. It believes in telling the facts of life and revealing the truths as they are discovered regardless of whose opinions it shocks. It is ever ready and willing to accept the new and discard the old. Atheism does not believe that man's mission on earth is to love and glorify God, but it does believe in living this life so that when you pass on, the world will be better for your having lived.

That is the ideal that now inspires more hearts to help humanity in its upward march than ever before in the history of the human race.

That is the ideal that inspired Shelley, that inspired Voltaire, and Humboldt, and Garibaldi; that inspired Mark Twain, and John Burroughs, and Luther Burbank. That is the ideal that inspires Sir Arthur Keith, Albert Einstein and Thomas A. Edison.

If man wants help he must abandon his appeals to God. They will prove only "echoes of his wailing cries."

The Evolution of Ideas

Atheism does not place any trust in God. The inscription on our coins is a lie.

It was not long since when a person who denied the existence of a personal god, who refused to accept the Bible as a divine revelation, who branded as absurd that Christ was miraculously conceived, who characterized as a delusion the resurrection, and who stigmatized as a myth immortality of the soul, was charged by ministers of religion with being an Atheist.

Thomas Paine was called a "filthy little atheist" upon evidence that he did not even approximate this.

To call oneself anything but a Freethinker or an Atheist after the denials of these religious premises is to belie one's own words.

We do not intend to let the clergy, to suit their fancy or their moods, give us our definition of Atheism.

It may be perfectly satisfactory for the editors of the Encyclopedia Britannica to commission a clergyman to write upon Atheism, but that is no reason why we should accept him as an authority.

If a clergyman knew enough about Atheism to write with authority upon the subject he would no longer remain a clergyman.

The rejection of religion and the denial of God has been the definition of Atheism from time immemorial. We have accepted it in the past, and we accept it today. We do not intend to compromise upon a single point.

If religionists have advanced to our position, it is they who must accept our banner.

PIETY CONDEMNS THOUGHT

Have we so soon forgotten the Scopes Trial when Evolution was denied a place in the school curriculum because it was branded as godless; when all Evolutionists were charged with being blasphemous atheists?

Atheism has given to the human race the intellectual monarchs of the world.

When the great Darwin discovered the law of the origin of species, he was called an Atheist because he disproved the special creation of Man.

THE STEPS OF SKEPTICISM

When the Chemist went into his laboratory and discovered the indestructibility of matter, he was called an Atheist because he proved the impossibility of a Creator.

When the Astronomer pointed his telescope to the sky and explored the regions of unlimited space, he was called an Atheist because he found no god within the confines of space and no heaven within the region of his explorations.

When the Geologist determined the age of the earth through its rock and soil and formations, he was called an Atheist because he too destroyed a belief in the special six-day creation and repudiated the biblical cosmogony.

When the Historian went back to ancient and prehistoric times and discovered civilizations of high ethical and moral culture, of intellectual achievements that are still an amazement to us, he was called an Atheist because he exposed the myth of Adam, uncovered the mistakes of Moses, and branded with the epithet of fraud the commands of Jehovah.

When the Physician sought to alleviate the pain and suffering of Man, he was called an Atheist because he refused to accept the existence of disease as a special visitation of a vengeful god.

Even the discovery of anesthesia, the most humane of all of man's accomplishments, was branded as an impious intrusion, and an effort to circumvent and defeat the so-called will of this monstrous creature. And Timothy Dwight, a gentleman, once president of Yale College, preached a sermon against vaccination on the ground that smallpox was a decree of God and it was a frightful sin to avoid it.

Every Scientist who refuses to be held back by narrow theological limitations, and searches Nature for her secrets, becomes an Atheist, the Millikans, the Osborns, and the Pupins to the contrary notwithstanding.

That electrical wizard, a Prometheus himself, the late Charles P. Steinmetz, said that Atheism was the ultimate philosophy of the scientists.

"Where there are three students of nature there are two Atheists," is an old saying.

INGERSOLL'S HIGH IDEAL

In this age and generation no one need cloak his Atheism with some garment of so-called "religious respectability."

Charles Bradlaugh's and Robert G. Ingersoll's fight to make Atheism respectable has fortunately come to pass.

When religion expresses a nobler sentiment than that contained in these words of Ingersoll's, then, and only then, might it assume a superior attitude. He said:

"Call me infidel, call me atheist, call me what you will, I intend to so treat my children that they can come to my grave and truthfully say, 'He who sleeps here never gave us one moment of pain. From his lips, now dust, never came to us an unkind word.'"

Compare that statement with the words of Jesus Christ when he said that if a man hate not his mother and his father, his brother and his sister, his wife and his children, he cannot become his disciple, and then decide whose mantle you prefer to wear!

THE DECLINE OF THEISM

In our own day we see a revolution taking place in the ranks of religion. We see the liberating force of the great Freethinkers of the past having their effects upon our generation by the breaking of the chains of superstition that have enslaved mankind to a degrading religion.

Our fight today is no longer against Theism. The arguments that were used by Freethinkers more than a century ago are now being used by the liberal minister against his more orthodox brother.

Who can deny that progress has been made when ministers themselves repudiate Theism?

Who today would expose himself to public ridicule and defend Theism in the face of its history and its record?

It has perverted the mentality of man and has caused him outrageously to abuse his own life.

In the name of God and for the love of God, Hell, in all its fury, was let loose upon the earth.

No wonder Theism is being repudiated and disowned.

The liberal minister will have none of it.

Like Caesar, "but yesterday it might have stood against the world, but now lies it here and none so poor as to do it reverence."

Even in our theological colleges, we see the impossibility of trying to harness a man of intelligence with the bridle of Theism, and as the result of this impossible combination, there is a widespread repudiation of religion and all that it stands for.

We are witnessing a period of intellectual honesty that does credit even to ministers of religion. There is a positive and an aggressive advance towards the ideals of Freethought.

THE DEATH OF MYTHS

And the time is not far distant when a minister who takes money for prayers for the repose of the so-called soul of man, will be charged with misrepresentation and fraud just as others are now being apprehended for similar schemes of deception.

When a minister today makes a public declaration that he can no longer believe in the Virgin Birth, the resurrection of

Christ, in the inspiration of the Scriptures; acknowledges that Moses was very often mistaken, and can find no justification for the existence of a personal god, the brass band plays and the flags wave for his "great courage," while as a matter of fact these things have been so obvious to us that we look with pity upon people who still believe them.

Full Way with Truth

We have no applause for those who have stolen the thunder from the leaders of Freethought only to cloak it in a garment of so-called "liberal religion."

We are encouraged at the progress they have made, but unless they come the full way, they must be watched with the same vigilance and fought with the same force as the Calvins and Knoxes.

Halfway measures will never do. They invariably prove futile.

What a complete revolution has taken place when people must make apologies for their religious beliefs, and give symbolical interpretations to the incomprehensible ravings of insane men! When they must deny and reject the beliefs that were but a few decades ago so tyranically imposed upon the people and for which unnumbered thousands suffered the penalty of torture and death!

The Bondage of Beliefs

Is the modern trend to perpetuate religion, or is it doomed to occupy the same place in history as the institution of slavery? And how apt is that comparison of religion with slavery!

Throughout the ages religion has imprisoned and chained and stultified the brain of man, just as the institution of slavery has bound and manacled and torn the limbs of man!

And when efforts were made to abolish the hateful institution of slavery there were many who by their compromises only prolonged its existence.

And the efforts of those today who are compromising with religion and making apologies for its past crimes, are only prolonging its existence and making more difficult the task to eradicate this blot upon civilization.

They are interfering with the removal of the worst obstacle that has ever blocked the intellectual progress of Man.

A rose may smell as sweet by any other name, and religion will be just as obnoxious under any other title.

There are some who claim that religion can be humanized, but how can we humanize something that does not admit of humanization?

How can we humanize ignorance, superstition and brutality? Can we humanize the thumb-screw, the rack and the auto da fé?

If we could humanize religion then the dream of the alchemist will have come true.

If we could humanize religion then truly base metal can be converted into gold.

Humanism and Unitarianism differ only in degree and not in kind from Catholicism and Presbyterianism. The great trouble with the liberal Unitarian, the Modernist and the Humanist is that we do not know where they stand. Their attachment to religion as an element of respectability is still an enigma. Their so-called emancipation from the fetishes and superstitions of their more orthodox brethren is more apparent than real.

Before the Board of Education of this city some years ago, when the proposal was made to permit children to receive religious training on public school time, the most fanatical supporter and most vehement proponent of this scheme was a Unitarian Minister.

He loudly decried the fact that our children were being "deprived" of a religious education. He stood side by side and shoulder to shoulder with Monsignor Lavelle of St. Patrick's Cathedral and the late Bishop Burch of the Protestant Episcopal Church.

Defense of Pious Fake

This minister was terribly perturbed because he was afraid our children would grow up without some knowledge of the story of Adam and Eve; that they would not be acquainted with Jonah's sojourn in the belly of the whale, or of the miraculous conversation of Baalam and his Ass.

And while Freethinkers were making an effort for the newspapers publicly to state, on their behalf, that they had offered a thousand dollars reward for the evidence of one authentic cure that took place at the grave of the consumptive priest, Father Patrick Powers, buried in the cemetery at Malden,

Massachusetts, Charles Francis Potter was making a declaration from the platform of his Humanist pulpit, concerning these so-called cures, that "there was something in it."

If it is Mr. Potter's contention that auto-suggestion has accomplished beneficial results in patients suffering from mental disorders, our answer is that we heartily approve of the application of mental therapy in such cases, but do not believe that it should be administered in a grave yard!

By his public statement he condoned this shameful exploitation of thousands of credulous people who were making a weary pilgrimage, at the sacrifice of their health, to this latest fraudulent undertaking of the church.

Immediately following Mr. Potter's statement, Gardner Jackson, writing in the *Nation*, exposed this pious fraud. Mr. Jackson very significantly showed the close blood relationship between the superintendent of the cemetery and Cardinal O'Connell of Boston. They were brothers! He also very vividly depicted the baskets of money that were being emptied as rapidly as the poor deluded creatures would fill them.

In our opinion, it was the duty of every American to use his efforts to prevent the establishment in this country of so barefaced a fraud as the establishment of a shrine similar to that of Lourdes which now disgraces France.

If to condone such a disgraceful exhibition as a gesture of compromise with religion is a sample of Humanism, then we want none of it!

Church Parasitism

And even John Haynes Holmes, for whom I have the highest personal regard, and who stands at the forefront of the liberal ministers of this country, cannot be pardoned for his advocacy of exempting church property from taxation. He claims that churches increase the property value of the surrounding buildings and permit the maximum of air and light.

I say that if you make a park out of the land upon which the church stands, you will accomplish all that Mr. Holmes claims for the church, and one thing more. It will do away with the evil of the church and free the country of these institutions of superstition and houses of stultification.

But with the advent of the skyscraper building on church property even this argument falls to the ground. The present tendency of the church is to get "under cover" of an income-producing apartment house or office building.

Let us replace the churches of this city with a system of parks and we will make New York the most beautiful, the most attractive and the most healthful city on the face of the earth.

Society has no right, through the instrumentality of its government, to exempt from taxation a single institution, while a member of the community is without food and shelter.

The church may be successful in convincing a person that the more he suffers here the less he will suffer hereafter, but we are concerned with putting food into his stomach, clothes on his back, and shelter over his head now.

One may believe what he will as long as he is well fed and protected from the elements, but the moment he falls below that condition he is actually deprived of food necessary to life by the church that does not pay taxes.

In reality it is actually stealing food from one who is starving.

It is like a miser counting his gold while poverty is knocking at his bolted door.

To delude a man into believing that the more he gives of the possessions of this life for the imaginary benefits to be enjoyed in a mythical one is to perpetrate upon him a monstrous and unforgivable fraud.

Every steeple that rises above a church is a dagger thrust into the heart of Humanity. It has proved so in the past. And by the past, we judge the future.

Present Trend Atheistic

The situation today is not whether the present trend in religion, with its impossible premises and its still more impossible articles of belief, leads to a compromise with science, or whether it should be liberalized into a respectable harmony with the pace set by education and the progress made by man, but whether its complete eradication must be accomplished so that it may no longer hamper man in his search for the truth nor be an obstacle in his path toward his ultimate mastery of the forces of Nature.

Only when a man ceases to be a child, only when he emancipates himself completely from the fetishes of religion, and gives up his silly and childish ideas concerning the existence of God, will he be able to rise to that commanding position and station in life when he can be truly called a Man!

LINCOLN
THE FREETHINKER

by

Joseph Lewis

Author of "The Tyranny of God," "The Bible Unmasked,"
"Burbank, the Infidel," "Jefferson, the Freethinker,"
"Atheism," "Franklin, the Freethinker," "Voltaire, the
Incomparable Infidel," "The Bible and the Public Schools,"
"Shall Children Receive Religious Instruction?" "Mexico
and the Church," "Spain: Land Blighted by Religion," etc.

THE FREETHOUGHT PRESS ASSOCIATION, INC.
317 EAST 34th STREET, NEW YORK, N. Y.

From the Laboratory
of
Thomas A. Edison,
Orange, N.J.

November 19, 1924.

The Lincoln Publishing Co.,
1658 Broadway,
New York City.

Gentlemen:

I wish to thank you for Mr. Lewis' book on "Lincoln
The Freethinker".

This is another of the many publications brought out
in late years which are dispelling the clouds of superstition
and breaking our bondage to a mythical religion.

Yours very truly,

Thos A Edison

A Photographic Facsimile of Edison's Letter Greatly Reduced in Size

Washington, _____, 186

Four score and seven years ago our fathers brought
forth, upon this continent, a new nation, conceived
in liberty, and dedicated to the proposition that
"all men are created equal"

Now we are engaged in a great civil war, testing
whether that nation, or any nation so conceived
and so dedicated, can long endure. We are met
on a great battle field of that war. We have
come to dedicate a portion of it, as a final resting place for those who died here, that the nation
might live. This we may, in all propriety do. But, in a
larger sense, we can not dedicate — we can not
consecrate — we can not hallow, this ground —
The brave men, living and dead, who struggled
here, have hallowed it, far above our poor power
to add or detract. The world will little note, nor long
remember what we say here, while it can never
forget what they did here.

It is rather for us, the living, we here be dedicated to the great task remaining before us —
that, from these honored dead we take increased devotion to that cause for which
they here, gave the last full measure of devotion — that we here highly resolve these
dead shall not have died in vain; that
the nation, shall have a new birth of freedom, and that government of the people by
the people for the people, shall not per-
ish from the earth

Facsimile (slightly reduced) of the original draft of Lincoln's Gettysburg
Address. The words "Under God" are not included. See text page 20.

Abraham Lincoln was, in my judgment, in many respects, the grandest man ever President of the United States. Upon his monument these words should be written: "Here sleeps the only man in the history of the world, who, having been clothed with almost absolute power, never abused it, except upon the side of mercy".

Robert G. Ingersoll.

LINCOLN, THE FREETHINKER *

I REMEMBER once reading a statement in the public press that no person could be elected President of the United States unless that person were a believer in the Christian religion. At the time I saw this statement I took it as being true, because there came to my mind a story often told about Robert G. Ingersoll.

The story was something like this:

A number of prominent men and women came to pay a visit to the celebrated orator and during the course of conversation one of them remarked that the Colonel had a magnificent library which was no doubt extremely expensive. To this Ingersoll replied, that his library *was* exceedingly expensive and possibly the most expensive library of any individual in the world. The questioner looked a bit dubious at the reply and ventured that he thought he had seen libraries which cost a great deal more than the Colonel's. In reply to this, Ingersoll said that *his* library cost him the presidency of the United States.

But it is not true that a person must be a believer in the Christian religion as a qualification to hold that high

* Address delivered at banquet of the Freethinkers' Society of New York on the evening of February 12th, 1924, at Hotel Belleclaire, 77th Street at Broadway, New York City.

and distinguished office. More than one President of this great country was a disbeliever in the Christian plan of salvation, and, peculiarly so, the very men who were not Christians have been acknowledged as the greatest in that long list of illustrious men who have received the highest gift within the power of this nation. Washington, Jefferson and Lincoln, all unbelievers, are the great triumvirate of the United States of America.

My effort, and it is a labor of love, is to show you tonight that Lincoln, that sad-eyed martyr of this Republic, was a Freethinker, "even as you and I." But in proving to you that Lincoln was a Freethinker, it becomes necessary to disprove the frequent assertion that he was a Christian. Under ordinary circumstances, it would not be necessary to prove a man was not something else in order to establish what he was. But in the case of Abraham Lincoln such a procedure is absolutely essential, because the Christian world, in a shameful disregard of the truth, claims an absolute monopoly of great men.

It is strange that very little effort is being made by the Christian world to prove the religious beliefs of Presidents other than those three who stand so preeminently as America's greatest statesmen; I think I can safely say that there are more volumes written to prove Lincoln a Christian than to prove the religious conviction of any other statesman of this country. And, like a man that "doth protest too much," there is a reason for this. Perhaps they are believers in the motto that if you tell a lie often enough you will begin to believe it yourself, and so hardly a year passes that a book by some clergyman proclaiming Lincoln a Christian, is not issued from the press.

Last year, in response to a public announcement that a prominent senator was to deliver an address on Lincoln, I attended this gathering. Through an unfortunate circumstance the senator was unable to attend, and the minister in charge of the ceremonies announced that in the evening, at his church, he would deliver an address upon "Lincoln, the Christian." But in making this announcement he seemed to apologize for his liberty in calling Lincoln a Christian without the proper evidence to support his contention, and quoted Emerson, by saying: "What you are speaks louder than what you say." Under those conditions you can prove anything to be anything you want to prove it to be. But we will measure Lincoln for not only what he said, but also for what he did not say. We will follow the motto that although "actions speak louder than words," only hypocrites say what they do not believe.

In order to be a Christian it is necessary to believe the Bible to be a divinely inspired book. To be a Freethinker it is essential that you reject the Bible as a revelation from God. To determine, then, whether a person is a Christian or a Freethinker should indeed be very simple. A person may believe in God and yet reject the Bible as a divine book. Such a person cannot be a Christian believer, but may be a Freethinker.

A person may believe in the Bible, and according to his particular interpretation be any one of the following divisional sects of Christianity: Catholic, Presbyterian, Methodist, Baptist, Episcopalian, Congregationalist, Seventh Day Adventist, Holy Roller or Holy Jumper.

A Freethinker may be any one of the following: A Deist, a Rationalist, a Pantheist, a Materialist, an Agnostic, or an Atheist.

It is not my intention to dispute with any particular branch of Christianity that may claim Lincoln as its follower, nor classify him in any one of the subdivisions by which a Freethinker may declare himself. It is my purpose to disprove that Lincoln was a Christian, and with the produced evidence, to show unequivocally, that he was an avowed Freethinker.

Evidence may be true or false. Proof of evidence is the only test of its reliability. The proof of a statement, without evidence, depends a great deal upon the person who makes it. What ministers say, particularly in religious controversies, requires corroboration.

For a great many years it was impossible to secure the "Life of Lincoln," as written by his intimate friend and law partner, William H. Herndon. And yet it was to Herndon, that Lincoln on becoming President, said that he wished his own name associated with that of Herndon's until death.

It seems that the religious world took exception to this "Life of Lincoln." It was found to contain too many truths that were not in harmony with the notions of a number of clergymen.

The story goes that every available copy of Herndon's

"Life of Lincoln" was purchased by the clergy, some paying as high as one hundred dollars for a copy. They did not spend this money for the book because of its intrinsic value; they did not want its facts known to the public. For nearly twenty-five years this work on Lincoln was held at a premium, and I believe it was only last year, in response to an overwhelming demand, that the descendants of Herndon decided upon a republication of the volumes, and they are, fortunately, once more available to the general public.

Herndon's "Life of Lincoln" is conceded by all fair-minded persons to be the most accurate picture of the life of the sixteenth President of this country that has ever been written. Some maintain that Herndon was to Lincoln what Boswell was to Johnson. Men prominent in the higher walks of life, members of Congress, Senators, Judges, members of the President's cabinet, intimate friends and relatives and even his wife, testify that Lincoln was an unbeliever, an infidel, a Freethinker. Strangers, a few casual acquaintances and a number of clergymen, known and unknown, maintain that he was a Christian. And yet the two ministers most intimately acquainted with Lincoln—Bishop Simpson and the Reverend P. D. Gurley—do not support the contention of their more zealous, but less truthful fellow "divines."

The weight of the evidence is so preponderantly in favor of Lincoln's religious emancipation that it seems almost impossible that anyone could be so audacious as to assert that he believed in any dogma of any religious denomination. But we cannot prevent anyone from saying what he will, particularly in religious matters, where the emotion stronger than reason, sometimes prompts the religious fanatic even to murder a person in an endeavor to "save his soul." It may seem a paradox, and yet in religious matters the things most difficult of performance are the things most easily believed. And for Christianity not to possess Lincoln as an adherent is truly a tragedy for it. It is a thrust too painful to bear. It is no small wonder, then, that some clergymen have stooped to questionable means and methods in their endeavors to show Lincoln to have been a member of their faith. They did not seek the truth. They strained every fact to the breaking point in their endeavor to find some shred upon which they might base their claim. But, alas! unable to secure any truthful evidence, some, as proof of their contention, have said that Lincoln possessed the virtues of Patience, Tenderness and Charity.

As though these were exclusively "Christian" virtues!

For ages the virtues of Christianity were exemplified in the heartlessness that murdered a Hypatia, and the cruelty that accompanied the Crusades; that schemed and inflicted the punishment of an inquisition; that burned a Bruno and imprisoned a Galileo; that madly and joyously took part in a Massacre of St. Bartholomew's Eve, and that with due solemnity judicially tried, and convicted, sentenced and executed a rooster for laying eggs!

It requires but little effort on the part of the unscrupulous to find witnesses to testify falsely. I remember distinctly that when I first read the claim that Thomas Paine recanted I was simply overwhelmed. I was not only convinced that this brave and good man recanted before he died, but I felt certain, from the charges brought against him, that he had led a most profligate and dissolute life. No doubt the defamers of Paine believed in the motto, that if you throw enough mud a little of it will stick. I was stunned and bewildered. I was sore at heart to feel that so great and unselfish a man, the author of the "Age of Reason" and the "Rights of Man," could have fallen to such miserable depths. But when I read Ingersoll's answer to the charges; when I saw how he disposed of each and every accusation; how he discredited the witnesses; how he exposed the character of the defamers and calumniators of Paine, I realized then that the reputation of any man with courage enough to speak the truth as he sees it may be besmirched if what he says is contrary to what the great mass of people are led to believe to be the truth.

I also realized then that the statement of a minister, especially in a bitter religious controversy, must be substantiated before being accepted as a verity. But "truth crushed to earth will rise again," and as it was with Paine, so it is with Lincoln.

Were the Civil War a failure, had the Union perished, the church would not be straining every muscle to claim Lincoln a believer in Christianity. Rather they would "shout from the house tops" the destruction brought upon this nation by the insane idealism of this arrogant infidel!

All the horrors of that war would be vividly pictured before you. They would relate with glee, how in early manhood he had written a pamphlet against the Bible and Christianity, and how, seated among others discussing its points, it was snatched from his hands and thrown into the fire. How they would dwell upon this act of "Providence"; and with a sanctimoniousness becoming only to Christians, they would pray God to save them from another Lincoln. Slavery would still be the topic of the Christian pulpit and the "divine institution" would still be supported by the Biblical edict: "Servants, be obedient to them that are your masters according to the flesh, with fear and trembling."

But the fact of the matter is that the manuscript that Lincoln wrote against the Bible and Christianity was taken from him and destroyed by a friend and fellow Freethinker, Samuel Hill, his employer, who feared the effects of such a book upon his public career. His friend knew the "liberality" of the religious-minded, and, *fortunately for the Republic, his manuscript perished and the Nation was saved!*

When Lincoln ran for Congress against the Reverend Peter Cartwright, charges were brought against him by clergymen that he was an infidel, and that he said that Christ was an illegitimate child. And not once did Lincoln deny the truth of these charges. When asked why he did not deny them, Lincoln said he did not do so for two reasons: First, he knew the charges to be true; and second, they could be easily proved.

Galileo became a heretic when he questioned the truth of Joshua's influence upon the sun. Were Charles Darwin a Christian, the "Origin of Species" would never have seen the light of day, and William Jennings Bryan would have been denied the great opportunity of making a monkey of himself. *And if Abraham Lincoln were a Christian, the emancipation of the Negro slaves would never have entered his mind!*

Slavery is just as much a fundamental part of Christianity as is the Virgin Birth. To contradict one is just as serious as to deny the other. Leviticus, Chapter 25, Verses 44 to 46, is just as much part of the Bible as are the Ten Commandments. If one is "inspired" so is the other, and I quote the former:

> "Both thy bondmen and thy bondmaids, which thou shalt have, shall be of the heathen round about you; of them ye shall buy bondmen and bondmaids. Moreover of the children of the strangers that do sojourn among you, which they begat in your land; and they shall be your possession. And ye shall take them as an inheritance for your children after you, to inherit them for a possession; they shall be your bondmen forever."

The following quotations from the New Testament require the same belief and acceptance from Christians as does the resurrection of Christ.

I quote Timothy, Chapter 1, Verse 1:

> "Let as many servants as are under the yoke count their masters worthy of all honor."

And Titus, Chapter 2, Verse 9:

> "Exhort servants to be obedient to their masters."

As proof that the emancipation of the Negro slaves was opposed by the Christian Church, I need but quote the testimony of the celebrated divines of that time.

The Reverend Alexander Campbell said: "There is not one verse in the Bible inhibiting slavery, but many regulating it. It is not then, we conclude, immoral."

The Reverend E. D. Simms, professor, Randolph-Macon College, wrote: "The extracts from Holy Writ unequivocally assert the right of property in slaves."

The Reverend R. Furman, D.D., Baptist, of South Carolina, said: "The right of holding slaves is clearly established in the Holy Scriptures, both by precept and example."

The Reverend Thomas Witherspoon, Presbyterian, of Alabama, said: "I draw my warrant from the Scriptures of the Old and New Testaments to hold the slave in bondage."

The Reverend Nathan Lord (what an authoritative name!), president of Dartmouth College, said: "Slavery was incorporated into the civil institutions of Moses; it was recognized accordingly by Christ and his apostles. *They condemned all intermeddlers with it.*"

The Reverend Taylor, principal of the Theological Department of Yale College (and he certainly ought to know), said: "I have no doubt that if Jesus Christ were on earth, he would, under certain circumstances, become a slaveholder." And I want to say here and now that I agree absolutely with the Reverend Gentleman.

And Lincoln himself said: "All the powers of the earth seem rapidly combining against the slave, Mammon is after him—and the theology of the day is fast joining in the cry."

But the most striking illustration of history, showing the close connection between the Bible and slavery, is the fact that when the Revolutionists of France—Freethinkers all—rejected the Bible as a state book of authority, they also abolished slavery throughout the French possessions. *And when the monarchist government came back into power, and the church regained control of the government, the Bible again became a state book of authority and the institution of slavery was re-established.*

To show the close connection between the belief in the Bible and the institution of slavery I need but mention the fact that when a bill was introduced in Parliament to abolish slavery in the British Empire, Lord Chancellor Thurlow characterized the move as "miserable and contemptible" and as being "contrary to the word of God."

And I repeat and re-emphasize, *that it was utterly impossible for Abraham Lincoln to be a believer in the Bible, and be the author of the Emancipation Proclamation.*

A Christian believes the Bible to be the infallible word of God. He believes that all the knowledge necessary to his well-being, happiness and immortality is contained therein. To question its precepts is heresy to him. It is because of this belief that Christianity has to its credit the Dark Ages. To doubt, to investigate, to improve, to advance, is a principle contrary to the doctrines of religion. "Prove all things, hold fast to that which is true," means to the religious-minded only what the Bible says is true. "Whatever is, is best," is the brake upon the wheel of progress. "God's will" is the stereotyped answer to all that is. If Lincoln were a Christian he would have accepted the Negro's plight in life as in accordance with the "divine plan" as enunciated in the "Holy Bible."

It was because Lincoln was not bound by any creed, not hampered by any religious belief, that he felt that the mark of the vicious lash upon the tender skin was not and could not be right by divine sanction, and for that reason he waged the most just war in humanity's heroic struggle for freedom. "In giving freedom to the slave, we assure freedom to the free," is the statement that no believer in the Bible could utter.

Even those clergymen who claim that Lincoln accepted Christianity in the latter years of his life, admit that in early manhood he was an infidel. His first law partner, John T. Stewart, said: "Lincoln was an avowed and open infidel, and sometimes bordered on Atheism. He went farther against Christian beliefs, doctrines and principles than any other man I ever heard."

The impression, now being created in the minds of our school children, that Lincoln's only sources of knowledge were the Bible and Pilgrim's Progress is, in view of the facts, a deliberate and malicious falsehood. Lincoln was a reader and lover of Voltaire, Volney and Paine, and was not satisfied with being enlightened himself, but informed others of what he had found out. He thought it miserly to keep that knowledge to himself and was zealous in his heresy. He argued and talked for that which he had discovered to be true. It is said that he never tired of reading Paine; and I ask, who does tire of reading him? Who can read the "Age of Reason" without being convinced by its logic?

Oh, what a valuable, what a priceless copy of the "Age of Reason" it was that fell into the hands of Abraham Lincoln! The germ of Lincoln the Emancipator was planted when he read these liberty-loving books. And friends, as a gentle reminder, if you have a son whom you would like to see develop into another Lincoln, you cannot better equip him than by giving him the same mental food upon which Abraham Lincoln thrived.

Lincoln's belief in "God" or "Providence" prompted him to say: "Friends, I agree with you in Providence, but I believe in the Providence of the most men, the largest purse and the longest cannon."

The use of the word "God" has a thousand interpretations and does not reveal the religious belief of the person using that word. The manner in which Lincoln used the word "God" in his immortal papers should be sufficient proof that he had no faith in the generally accepted sense of that word. I think the following incident as related by Herndon should settle for all time the significance of the use of the word "God" by Lincoln. "No man had a stronger or firmer faith in Providence than Lincoln, but the continued use by him late in life of the word 'God' must not be interpreted to mean that he believed in a personal God. In 1854 he asked me to erase the word 'God' from a speech I had written and read to him for criticism, because my language indicated a personal God, whereas, he insisted, no such personality existed."

Herndon goes farther and says: "If Lincoln were asked whether he believed in God, he would have said: 'I do not know that a God exists.'"

Lincoln's two most important documents, the Emancipation Proclamation and the Gettysburg Address, were originally written with the idea of God completely left out. It is an historical fact and noteworthy to us that the Emancipation Proclamation was written and printed by Lincoln before he consulted the members of his cabinet. When he called them into conference he handed each a copy, and asked them for any suggestions. One member, the Honorable Salmon P. Chase, after reading it, stated:

> "Mr. Lincoln, this paper is of the utmost importance—greater than any state paper ever made by this government. A paper of so much importance, and involving the liberties of so many people, ought, I think, to make some reference to the Deity. I do not observe anything of the kind in it."

"No, I overlooked it," replied Lincoln. "Won't you make a draft of what *you* think *ought* to be inserted?"

And the following words as suggested by the Honorable Salmon P. Chase were inserted in the proclamation:

"I invoke the considerate judgment of mankind and the gracious favor of Almighty God."

No doubt a similar circumstance was responsible for the words "under God" being put into the Gettysburg Address as the original draft of this immortal speech makes no mention of these words.*

* See facsimile reproduction on page 4.

We must not lose sight of the fact that Lincoln was the most misunderstood and hated man of his day. There were conspirators in every branch of the Government, and, it has been intimated, even in his own cabinet. We must not judge him for what he permitted others to do in order to accomplish his glorious undertaking, and if the churches of his day were ready to strike him down on the slightest provocation, the oversentimental references to "God" in his messages can be readily understood as of little importance.

When chided about his Thanksgiving messages as being contrary to his known convictions on the subject, Lincoln said to Judge James N. Nelson: "Oh! this is some of Seward's nonsense and it pleases the fools!" Lincoln knew the power of the church's hostility, and was a compromiser in the sense that he believed in "doing a little harm for a great good," particularly so when the end meant the liberation of thousands of human beings from the bondage of slavery. To the church, it is more important to crush the infidel than to add a step of progress to civilization and for that reason, while president, Lincoln was reticent in public upon the question of religion. By this act of discretion he carried the nation safely through the most trying period of its history.

It is very curious indeed, that if Lincoln were a Christian, as some say, nowhere in any of his writings does there appear a single mention of Jesus Christ. In his public addresses, official documents and his private correspondence, never once did he express a belief in any doctrine that would even remotely claim him as a Christian. On the contrary, his personal conversations were such as unhesitatingly to classify him an avowed Free-thinker. And yet some have the impudence to say that on the presentation of a $500 Bible, which some misguided Negroes of Baltimore gave him as a token of gratitude, he is quoted as saying:

> "In regard to the great book I have only this to say, that it is the best gift which God has given to Man. All the good from the Saviour of the world is communicated to us through this book. But for this book we could not know right from wrong. All those things desirable to man are contained in it."

This statement is a lie, the enormity of which I am unable to express. To say that Lincoln said this is too ridiculous for notice, and yet when uttered by a clergyman it is taken to be true. It is utterly impossible that Lincoln, who openly doubted the truth of the Bible and questioned the legitimacy of the birth of Christ, should utter such a puerile statement, especially to a group of people representing a race that had been so mercilessly subjected to a condition of servitude because of the Bible's precepts. Out of courtesy, Lincoln may have thanked the little group of well-meaning Negroes for their gift, yet thinking in his heart what fools they were to take $500 of their heard-earned money and waste it upon the *very instrument that was the greatest obstacle in their struggle for emancipation.*

More likely, sad-hearted Lincoln felt, if he did not actually say: "What fools you are; here I am striving with all the energy I possess, with the resources of a great

nation, sacrificing thousands of lives, the very flower of
the Republic, to liberate you from the chains of slavery,
and here you are presenting me with a Bible, a book
that has held the minds of men in mental slavery for over
a thousand years and has caused more mischief and heart-
ache, and agony and hatred and bloodshed than any other
instrument in the world.   Go; you are now physically
free: strive for mental emancipation."

Regarding this supposed speech to the group of Colored
People, permit me to quote Herndon concerning it:

> "I am aware of the fraud committed on Mr. Lincoln in
> reporting some insane remarks supposed to have been made by
> him, in 1864, on the presentation of a Bible to him by the
> colored people of Baltimore. *No sane man ever uttered such
> folly* and *no sane man will believe it.* In that speech Mr.
> Lincoln is made to say: 'but for this book we could not know
> right from wrong.' Does any human being believe that Lincoln
> ever uttered this? What did the whole race of Man do to know
> right from wrong during the countless years that passed before
> the book was written? How did the struggling race of Mankind
> build up its grand civilization in the world before this book was
> given to Mankind? What do the millions of people now living,
> who never heard of this book, do to know how to distinguish
> right from wrong? Was Lincoln a fool, an ass, a hypocrite, or
> a combination of them all? Or is this speech—*this supposed,
> this fraudulent speech—a lie?*"

Herndon's characterization of this supposed speech of
Lincoln to the negroes of Baltimore as a lie is the only
term that can properly be applied to it. It only goes to
prove to what lengths people will go in their desperation
to prove a false contention.

But one lie begets another and the great task before us
is to disprove them and halt their circulation. I believe
it was Mark Twain—another Freethinker, by the way—
who said that a lie could get into circulation and around

the world before truth had time to put on its shoes. While Lincoln was alive no one presumed to call him a Christian. His enemies took particular delight in referring to him as an infidel. And now that he is dead, we take it upon ourselves to defend his infidelity, if you please. And when I hear the word "infidel" used as anathema, I feel like answering, with all the sauciness of a child: "Sticks and stones will break my bones, but *names* will never hurt me."

Abraham Lincoln is *no less* Abraham Lincoln because he was a Freethinker. In fact, many of the world's greatest geniuses and benefactors have been Freethinkers. And it seems to me a very difficult thing sometimes to determine whether a person is a genius because he is a Freethinker or a Freethinker because he is a genius.

For years there has been circulated by the religious forces a picture of Lincoln with his son Tad standing beside him. Both are looking at a large book which Mr. Lincoln has in his lap. This picture is generally captioned: "Lincoln Reading the Bible to His Son." On close examination the book is discovered to be a picture album. And in a recent issue of a magazine in which this picture appeared, Ida M. Tarbell is the authority for the statement, that when this picture of Lincoln was taken he issued this injunction: "Now don't let anybody entitle this picture, 'The President Reading the Bible to His Son.'" How well have the religious forces carried out his wishes!

The following explanation from the *Boston Globe* has an interesting bearing upon this point.

"The pretty little story about the picture of President Lincoln and his son Tad, reading the Bible, is now corrected for the one hundredth time. The 'Bible' was Photographer Brady's *picture album* which the President was examining with his son while some ladies stood by. The artist begged the President to remain quiet and the picture was taken. The truth is better than fiction, even if the recital conflicts with a pleasing theory."

If the religious forces will go so far as to declare that a picture album is a Bible, what kind of other evidence would you expect them to present in order to prove their claim.

How can anyone say that Lincoln believed in the Bible when he so aptly characterized the religious forces of both the North and the South, by saying: "Both read the same Bible and pray to the same God, and each invokes his aid against the other." The opinion of the church element toward Lincoln and the reason for its opposition can best be told my Lincoln himself. In 1843 Lincoln desired a nomination for Congress and did all in his power to secure it. The opposition toward him was growing stronger and stronger and in a letter to some of his constituents he wrote as follows:

"The strangest combination of church influence was against me. Baker, (his opponent) was a Campbellite, and therefore *got all that church.* My wife has some relations in the Presbyterian church and some with the Episcopalian churches, and therefore *whenever it would tell, I was set down as either ONE OR THE OTHER, while it was everywhere contended that NO CHRISTIAN ought to vote for me because I BELONGED TO NO CHURCH and was suspected as being a deist.*"

On another occasion he is quoted as having made this laconic, and all too significant statement: "The Bible is not my book nor Christianity my profession."

The Honorable David Davis, a judge of the Circuit Court of Illinois, at the time that Lincoln was a practicing attorney, and who was Lincoln's intimate friend and adviser, and who later became a Supreme Court Judge of the state of Illinois—a United States Senator—a Vice-President of the United States and finally a member of that august body, the Supreme Court of the United States, has something to say regarding Lincoln's beliefs. The intimacy between Lincoln and Judge Davis was such a bond of friendship that upon Lincoln's death Judge Davis was chosen by common consent to be administrator of his estate. Few men of this country have been held in higher esteem by their contemporaries than was Judge Davis. Surely his years of association, his friendship and his intimacy with Lincoln qualify him to testify to Lincoln's religious convictions. Judge Davis says: "Lincoln had no faith in the *Christian* sense of the term—he had faith in law, principles, causes and effects."

Recently there appeared in this city a magnificent production of a play by John Drinkwater, entitled, "Lincoln." In that play Lincoln's life was beautifully portrayed, with the exception of one particularly great blunder, a blunder that adds little credit to the playwright. In this play Lincoln is shown in a humiliating position, and despite a letter from me correcting this falsity, the scene remained unchanged. In this play Lincoln is made to fall upon his knees in prayer. I emphatically state that no evidence exists that the grown Abraham Lincoln ever prostrated himself in prayer. The scene is a lie and belongs in the same category as that of Washington praying at Valley Forge. We need no better proof of the falsity of this scene regarding Lincoln than Lincoln himself when he said "What is to be will be, and no prayers of ours can arrest the decree."

In every great crisis there are always religious fanatics who have spoken directly to God, and who are directed by God to deliver certain messages. The Civil War was no exception, and Lincoln was not free from such annoyers. It is said that Lincoln, more than any other President, was constantly pestered by clergymen with advice from "divine sources." He controlled his temper only because of his sympathy for the mentally deranged. To indicate his attitude toward such people I will quote his words of contempt for them:

> "I am approached with the most opposite opinions and advice, and by religious men who are certain they represent the Divine Will. I hope it will not be irreverent in me to say, that if it is probable that God would reveal His will to others, on a point so connected with my duty, it might be supposed *He would reveal it directly to me.*"

On another occasion when a woman came to see Lincoln, claiming that God sent her to deliver His message of advice to him, he caustically replied to her as only a Free-thinker would:

> "I have neither the time nor disposition to enter into a discussion with the Friend, and will end this occasion by suggesting to her the question, whether, if it be true that the Lord has appointed me to do the work she has indicated, is it not probable that he would have communicated knowledge of the fact to me as well as to her?"

It is sometimes very difficult to determine properly whether these "very religious people" are not fit subjects for the lunatic asylum, and I wonder if this thought was in Lincoln's mind when he said: "When an individual in a church, or out of it, becomes dangerous to the public interest he must be checked."

Lincoln's real opinion of the clergy may be gathered from one of his anecdotes which, it is said, he delighted to repeat:

> "Once in Springfield, I was off on a short journey, and reached the depot a little ahead of time. Leaning against the fence just outside the depot was a little darky boy, whom I knew, named Dick, busily digging with his toe in a mud puddle. As I came up I said: 'Dick, what are you about?' Said he, 'Making a church.' Said I, 'What do you mean?' 'Why, yes,' said Dick, pointing with his toe, 'don't you see, there is the shape of it, there's the steps and the front, here's the pews, where the folks set and there's the pulpit.' 'Yes, I see,' said I, 'but why don't you make a minister?' 'Laws,' answered Dick, with a grin, 'I hain't got MUD enough for dat.'"

During the course of my address I mentioned the fact that during the latter years of his life Lincoln did not engage in prayer. I want to correct that statement. I want to retract it. For I do find that he did indulge in this form of religious exercise. While at the White House some one came to pay him a visit. A terrific storm was raging. It was raining and thundering with fearful intensity. His visitor found himself unable to leave. Lincoln reflected for a moment and with solemn reverence said: "O Lord, if it's all the same to you, give us a little *more light* and a little *less noise*." On another occasion Lincoln prayed to God with deep and reverent devotion, that He put stockings on the chicken's feet in winter.

More significant than anything that might be said by others on the subject of Lincoln's religious belief is the attitude of Lincoln himself toward religion. *The mere fact that he did not become a member of any church is alone sufficient to silence forever any charge that he was a Christian believer.*

Lincoln weighted down with the pains and burdens of the bloody struggle of the Civil War and with Death constantly staring him in the face, uttered the most important and striking testimony to his lifelong disbelief. It is irrefutable! In answer to a letter from Judge J. A. Wakefield, an old friend, inquiring and hoping that he had changed the infidel opinions and convictions of his early manhood, Lincoln wrote—and it is significant that this letter was written after the death of his son Willie:—

> "My earlier views of the unsoundness of the Christian scheme of salvation and the human origin of the scriptures, have *become clearer* and stronger with advancing years and I see no reason for thinking *I shall ever change them.*"

He emphatically denied the existence of Hell and with equal fervency said that if there were a God *all* would be saved or *none*. Lincoln certainly was not as godly as Jehovah, but his humanity was a thousand times greater. He delighted in repeating this homely, yet philosophic epitaph:

> "Here lies poor Johnny Kongapod,
> Have mercy on him, gracious God,
> *As he would do if he were God*
> And you were Johnny Kongapod."

Other evidence, equally striking and abundant can be adduced further to disprove the clergy's claim; but enough, I think, has been presented to settle beyond the peradventure of a doubt that Lincoln was not a Christian believer. And yet of the utmost significance is the fact that Mrs. Lincoln was a member and regular attendant of the Christian church and that Lincoln rarely attended the services with her. And like a thunderbolt to the heart of the Christian world, Mrs. Lincoln herself testifies that her illustrious husband and one of America's greatest presidents was a disbeliever in the Christian religion. Mrs. Lincoln says: "He never joined a church. He was not a technical Christian. He had no hope or faith in the usual acceptation of those words."

No effort of mine is needed to establish Lincoln's place in the glittering galaxy of the world's great immortals and humanitarians and if there is a resting place for those who have passed on, he is happily in company with Voltaire, Paine and Ingersoll. In lauding Lincoln as a Christian example, the church makes its own weapon and stabs itself with the very instrument it would use against us.

Abraham Lincoln belonged to no sect; he professed no creed; he was truly an American! We honor him as one of the foremost statesmen of this country.

We honor him as the Preserver of our Republic.

We honor him as the Great Emancipator, and we honor ourselves when we honor him as a fellow Freethinker.

APPENDIX

Since the publication of "Lincoln the Freethinker" there has been a widespread controversy regarding the authenticity of the famous Bixby letter which Lincoln was supposed to have written to Mrs. Lydie Bixby, of Boston, offering his condolence on the loss of her five sons in the Civil War, and in which he refers to "our Heavenly Father."

The true facts now brought to light concerning this letter are: that five sons of Mrs. Bixby were not killed in the Civil War, but only two sons; that almost every circumstance connected with the writing of this letter is now a matter of much speculation and doubt; that the men responsible for making the alleged facts public have been proved to be of questionable veracity, and that the original letter (if Lincoln ever wrote such a letter, which I doubt very much) is *not* in existence!

"Facsimiles are abundant and though they vary slightly," as stated by Dr. William E. Barton, in defense of the genuineness of this letter, is to me conclusive evidence that the "Bixby Letter" is but another pious fraud perpetrated upon our martyred President. For how would it be possible for facsimiles that "vary slightly" to be made from an original letter if it were not in existence? Furthermore, if such a letter ever existed, how could facsimiles that "vary slightly" be made from it, if they were facsimiles?

LINCOLN THE SOLDIER

By Joseph Lewis

*Address delivered over Radio Station WGBS,
New York City, February 12, 1925*

———

No one will deny the courage of the uniformed soldier who goes forth to battle. Neither will any one withhold from him the credit and respect to which he is entitled. But not all soldiers wear uniforms. Neither do all soldiers die upon the battle-fields 'mid shot and shell.

There are soldiers who do not know how to operate a gun; who do not go forth to battle amid the beating of drums, the waving of flags or the cheering of people.

There are soldiers who fight, not upon the battle-fields, but upon the field of thought. Upon the battle-field there is somewhat of an equal contest. Man power can be met with man power and destructive explosives with devastating projectiles. But infinitely more courage and superior ammunition are required to do battle in the larger arena of human action.

The progress of mankind has been one bitter struggle against the forces of reaction; a battle of herculean effort against invisible and deadly enemies.

On the battle-field, the roaring of guns and the bursting of shells are a signal that the enemy is approaching and preparation is made by the defending army to withstand the attack; but in the battle for human progress, the enemy gives no such signs of approach.

Ignorance, Hatred, and Superstition are the malignant enemies of the human race. These vicious enemies do not fight in open fields. They do not fight fairly. With them equal combat is unknown. Their victories are won in the dark. Stealth and hypocrisy are their weapons.

Thousands have died, millions have died in mortal combat upon the battle-fields in defense of their country, in defense of their homes, in behalf of liberty.

And thousands, yes millions, have died in that grand army of human progress,—soldiers in the army of Science, of Art, of Medicine, of Invention and Discovery, and in the army of Justice and Freedom.

The world is ever ready to do homage to the soldier upon the battle-field. But in the realm of human progress it is lamentably true that only too often does the gallant soldier receive rebuke and calumny for his reward.

Seldom, in his own day, does the soldier who fights for liberty taste the fruits of his victory.

Abraham Lincoln, the Soul of America, was a soldier in both of these armies. He donned a uniform, shouldered a gun, and marched to battle in defense of his country. He suffered the hardships and endured the trials of a soldier's life. As captain of a regiment in the Black Hawk War in 1832, Lincoln acquitted himself with honor. And upon his return from battle he received the plaudits of his countrymen.

War brutalizes our natures and hardens our hearts; it warps our thoughts and makes us callous to the sufferings of human life.

But Lincoln never permitted war to harden his heart nor stunt his feelings. He was possessed of a rare love for humanity. His kindliness knew no bounds and his honesty was so widespread that he was affectionately known as "Honest Abe." There were many who chided him for his "softheartedness," but Lincoln was *Lincoln* and was not to be swayed from his convictions.

Lincoln's soul was touched with the kinship of life by the magic wand of a mother's love. To Lincoln his mother was his Star of Hope, his Rainbow of Life, the myriad-colored arch that ever beckoned him to "carry on." Lucky indeed is the child whose mother inspires him with humanitarian ideas and thoughts and with the urge that he may so live that when he passes on the world will be better for his having lived.

Lincoln never forgot the lowliness from which he came and it was the memory of his hardships which caused him never to abuse his power except on the side of mercy.

You remember the case of William Scott? While Scott was on sentry duty, after a strenuous day of fighting, and exhausted from the wear and tear of battle, his strength failed him and he fell prostrate upon the ground. When discovered by another soldier and awakened, it was revealed that he was dreaming of his mother, and that she had awakened him to remind him of his duty as a soldier!

But in time of war, excuses for being asleep while on sentry duty are not acceptable or valid, and Scott was taken to his superior officer, tried by court-martial, convicted and condemned to be shot!

The case was brought to Lincoln's attention. His heart was touched. He could not make himself believe that the boy was a traitor, and ordered his release. You know what followed: Scott died fighting valiantly for the cause!

On another occasion a woman went to the White House and begged an audience with the President. Her husband had been captured, tried, convicted and was to be shot. Lincoln consented to see her. She told her story and pleaded with the President to suspend judgment. Lincoln asked her whether her husband was a good man and whether he treated her children kindly. She replied that he was a good husband and a good father and that the family could not live without him. She said he was a fool about politics and if she ever got him home he would do no more fighting for the South. "Well," said Lincoln, "I will pardon your husband and turn him over to you for safe keeping." The poor woman, overcome with joy, sobbed as though her heart would break. "My dear woman," said Lincoln, "if I had known how badly it was going to make you feel, I never would have pardoned him." "You don't understand," cried the woman between her sobs. "You don't understand, Mr. Lincoln." "Yes, yes, I do," answered the President, "and if you do not go away at once I shall be crying with you."

In our thoughts of Lincoln let us not forget that he was a human being, born just as you and I were born, only that his hardships were immeasurably greater than ours, his difficulties far more numerous. He had to struggle for everything he possessed. He had no teachers. He was self-taught. Tramping through the woods for six miles to borrow a grammar is an indication of his thirst for knowledge and the obstacles he overcame to acquire it.

He had an unquenchable desire to learn. A burning urge to accomplish. This urge prompted him to read every book he could get. He was once asked what he was reading, and he replied: "I'm not reading—I'm studying." He was particularly fond of controversies. He loved an argument. He was never satisfied unless the sparks flew in the discussions. "Hew to the block, let the chips fly where they will," was his motto. And fortunately this trait of Lincoln's broke down all barriers and prejudice in seeking knowledge. He was carried on the wave of Rationalism which swept this country in the Forties. This brought him in contact with the writings of Voltaire, Volney and Paine. They were his intimates.

Voltaire had shot his bolts at the caste system of Europe and the chains began to fall from the minds and bodies of men.

Thomas Paine was the first man on the American continent to raise his voice in behalf of the negro slaves.

Fired by these men with the love of Liberty and human rights, Abraham Lincoln entered the Army of Progress.

I see him on a flat boat navigating down the Mississippi River. I see him arrive at New Orleans. I see him in company with two friends come upon the market place. I see him watch the sale of a negro slave girl. I see him rebel at the revolting scene. As the girl is examined by her bidders, her flesh pinched, her form displayed, her nudity exposed, I see his sad face become more sorrowful, I see him clench his fist, and with a quiver in his voice, and an oath upon his lips, utter this statement: "If I ever get a chance to hit that thing [meaning slavery], I'll hit it hard." On his return to Springfield I see him enter the political arena with a short but crude declaration only to be concluded by that everlasting monument to his name, the Emancipation Proclamation. I now see him competing for public office. I see him defeated, halted in his march. But defeat and discouragement were words not to be found in Lincoln's vocabulary. When questioned concerning his defeat he said be felt like the boy who was too big to cry and too hurt to laugh. Determination was the quality of Lincoln's character and he knew that "the harder the struggle the more glorious the triumph," and so we see him overcoming the obstacles which had beset his path.

We now see him in his famous debates with Douglass, determining whether the nation can remain "half slave and half free," and whether "a house divided against itself can stand." And in this struggle let us not lose sight of the fact that Lincoln received the brunt of the battle. He was the most misunderstood and hated man of his day. The people did not welcome the economic and social changes which he advocated. The vilest of arguments were used against him. Arguments now known to be utterly ludicrous. He was vilified. He was slandered. The churches of his day opposed him and bigotry supported their contention. Let us take a lesson from the way Lincoln was treated and be not too ready to dismiss a new idea or condemn a new proposal.

In his fight for human emancipation he met the bitterest foes of battle. But not once did he falter, not once did he swerve. He had tasted battle as a soldier fighting for human rights against an institution whose only strength was that it was supported by "divine right." But Lincoln knew that man had no property right in man, and that the marks of the vicious lash upon the tender skin were not and could not be right by divine sanction, and that the damnable institution of slavery was a living lie against our Declaration of Independence!

We see Lincoln gaining in his struggle. We see a convention assembled. We see him nominated for President by an almost unanimous acclamation! We see him at the head of the Republic, Commander-in-Chief of its army, to determine "whether this nation, or any nation conceived in liberty and dedicated to the proposition that all men are created equal can long endure!"

We see him appealing for support—appealing to the nation's men to fight for the battle of freedom. After many anxious and uncertain moments we hear the mur-

mur of footsteps and the beating of drums and the welcome exclamation: "We are coming Father Abraham, we are coming 300,000 strong!"

And we see Lincoln, this giant of a man, who was too big to cry and too hurt to laugh, weeping for joy at the triumph that 3,000,000 human beings were to be released from the shackles of bondage; weeping for joy that the American Flag, the symbol of Liberty, was to rise once more over a united nation without a blemish and without a stain!

It is the duty of the soldier upon the battle-field to carry the flag of the country for which he fights, and if perchance he is shot and wounded and falls, another soldier must lift it from his hands and carry it high to battle, and this was the task delegated to Lincoln. He carried the flag of freedom which the American Revolutionists had given to Washington, and just as victory was won, just as he crossed the line with the flag waving high, this grand man, this soldier of the Republic, this Liberator, was struck down in battle and died that millions might be free!

Upon the grave of Lincoln, the military soldier, let us drop flowers of gratitude, and upon the brow of Lincoln the Emancipator, the soldier in the Army of Liberty, let us place a wreath as a symbol of the everlasting love and thanks of the human race.

JEFFERSON
THE FREETHINKER

by

Joseph Lewis

Author of "The Tyranny of God," "The Bible Unmasked,"
"Lincoln, the Freethinker," "Burbank, the Infidel," "Atheism," "Franklin, the Freethinker," "Voltaire, the Incomparable Infidel," "The Bible and the Public Schools," "Shall Children Receive Religious Instruction?" "Mexico and the Church," "Spain: Land Blighted by Religion," etc.

THE FREETHOUGHT PRESS ASSOCIATION, INC.
317 EAST 34th STREET, NEW YORK, N. Y.

JEFFERSON, THE FREETHINKER *

HERESY is still the greatest crime in the catalogue of man's misdeeds. You may be guilty of theft, you may be judged a forger, you may be socially and morally a brute and a reprobate, you may be a child beater and a wife deserter, aye, even a murderer, but with it all, if you are a religious believer, if you are "one of the fold," you may still have the respect of your friends, loyal supporters and heroic defenders. No matter how honest you may be, no matter how noble your character, or the loyalty of your bond and the sacredness of your word; no matter what intellectual achievements you may have attained, or accomplishments effected for the common good, if you are mentally above the rabble; if you have the courage of your convictions and exercise your prerogative of free speech and tell the world your honest thoughts; if you insist that ignorance and superstition should not usurp the throne of authority, you will be guilty of heresy, and conviction carries with it the stern sentence of ostracism.

It is needless for me to tell you, that of the men most responsible for the establishment of our Republic—both

* Address delivered by Joseph Lewis at banquet of the Freethinkers' Society of New York on the evening of April 13th, 1925, at Hotel Belleclaire, 77th Street and Broadway, New York City, in honor of the 182nd anniversary of the birth of Thomas Jefferson.—Also delivered over Radio Station W.G.B.S., October 8th, 1925.

in principle and in fact—Thomas Paine stands in the very forefront; and that because of his heresy, because of the expression of his religious conviction, due recognition and a rightful place in the niche of America has been denied this author-hero of our country.

And on a par with Thomas Paine as one of the early patriots of the Revolution, and as a brother infidel, stands Thomas Jefferson.

Were it not for the fact Thomas Jefferson held high governmental positions in the Republic—from that of the governorship of a state to the presidency of the Nation— he would to-day be suffering from lack of recognition of his services in the cause of Freedom, to the same degree that the author of "The Age of Reason" and "The Rights of Man" has endured for more than 100 years.

The great triumvirate of America, the three men upon whose brows rests the glory of the conflict, one in actual military duty, and all three in the intellectual battle for independence—are Benjamin Franklin, Thomas Paine, and Thomas Jefferson. Were it not for these three men, the Republic would never have been established and George Washington could not have been the first president of the United States of America.

Mighty may be your triumphs, noteworthy your achievements, honorable your conduct, spotless your character, but if you commit the unpardonable sin, if in religious matters you are a heretic, an infidel, an unbeliever, a freethinker, you will be, like Caesar upon his bier: "But yesterday, you might have stood against the world, but now lie you here and none so poor to do you reverence."

The passion of Jefferson's soul was Liberty. His torch

burned brightly with the fire of freedom. He could not see man as Man until he saw him mentally and politically free. He knew that the oppression of tyrant kings and the shackles of slavery were the milder forms of subjection under which man was made to suffer. He knew that mental bondage, slavery to superstition and fear, were the greatest obstacles to the emancipation of man. Jefferson had vision enough and forethought enough and intelligence enough to know that when man became mentally free, the shackles of all other forms of slavery would inevitably fall from his side. Once man was emancipated from degrading and enslaving superstitions, once free of the fears of religion, then priests could not beguile him nor governments enslave him; and then prejudice, that poisonous viper of human life, would be obliterated forever.

The grandest law that was ever written upon the Statute books of this or any other nation is the Statute of Religious Freedom which Jefferson drafted for the Virginia Constitution. Until the enactment of this provision for liberty of conscience, anyone who denied the existence of God, or the Trinity, or the Bible to be of Divine authority, was not permitted to hold civil or military office and was subjected to every penalty that an ignorant and vicious hierarchy could inflict. A father was even denied the custody of his own children.

But Jefferson knew that if the American Colonies were to prosper both as a government and as a nation, there must be a complete separation of Church and State. He knew that a church, supported by the State, was an enemy to man, whether it existed under a monarchy or under a

Republic. The injustice was the same, and bloodshed and disruption would be the result.

For eight long and tedious years he faced the united opposition of ignorance and bigotry and intrenched superstition. He silently endured the vilification and calumny of his enemies; and when victory was won and the Statute of Religious Freedom was enacted, a new dawn and a new day brightened upon the land, not only for America, but also for the world.

The United States became the intellectual haven for mankind. And only a man of the mental grandeur of Jefferson could have conceived and developed and formulated so broad and so magnificent a provision for freedom of thought. What Thomas Paine did as an individual and as a citizen, Thomas Jefferson accomplished as an official and as an executive.

Jefferson believed in the aristocracy of the mind, but in the democracy of man. Some of the other leaders of the Revolution believed in the aristocracy of man and in the democracy of mind. They believed that a select few should be the leaders and the rulers of the masses, and that the masses should believe all that the leaders and rulers dictated. Jefferson believed that the masses should possess the power of government, and that the individual should be the master of his mind.

Washington and Hamilton, particularly, strove for the establishment of the aristocracy of government and went so far as to favor the establishment of a state church. Jefferson knew that as long as the church had the support of the state it would usurp the right to regulate the people's lives, and that all forms of despotism and tyranny, with their attendant horrors of persecution and torture, would follow.

Jefferson knew, and felt no hesitation in saying, that "millions of innocent men and women, since the introduction of Christianity, have been burnt, tortured, fined and imprisoned; yet we have not advanced one inch towards uniformity. What has been the effect of coercion" he asked; "to make one half of the world fools and the other half hypocrites?"

He did not want an Inquisition in America—he looked with horror upon those instruments of torture which had so torn and mutilated the tender flesh of man.

He knew that the church and the priests could not be trusted with the people's sacred rights of freedom, and said: "In every country and in every age the priest has been hostile to liberty, he is always in alliance with the despot, abetting his abuses in return for protection to his own. It is error alone that needs the support of government. *Truth can stand by itself.*"

Armed with these facts and with undiminished courage, Jefferson defeated the efforts of Washington and Hamilton, and to his everlasting credit, to the everlasting benefit of this country, no state church was established. And were it not for Thomas Jefferson—and I say this after a full and thorough analysis of the facts at my disposal—this country to-day would not be a Republic.

Jefferson not only thwarted the efforts of Hamilton and others to establish a state church, but he also thwarted their efforts to establish an aristocracy. It was through the efforts of Thomas Jefferson that the first ten amendments, the very bulwark of our liberties, famous as the

Bill of Rights, were incorporated in our Federal Constitution. It was Jefferson—equally as successful as Lincoln—who preserved the Union; Lincoln from Secession and Jefferson from Aristocracy; one in an intellectual battle, the other in a military one. And, like Lincoln, during his political campaign, Jefferson had to contend with the accusation of being an Infidel.

The administration of Thomas Jefferson, the third President of the United States, was from every viewpoint and angle, the most nearly perfect of any administration during the Republic's existence. He was president in fact as well as in name; in practice as well as in principle.

He did not fight for a principle, and then violate that principle to please the ignorant. His Statute for Religious Liberty was not a popular campaign issue. He cared more for intellectual honesty and the sacredness of his oath, than for social or political favors. He was not to be cowed by religious bigots who had done their utmost, by threats of vituperation, to silence his tongue and direct his actions.

When he took the oath of office he swore to uphold the Constitution and he was not to break his oath for the benefit of either the selfish, the ignorant or the hypocritical; and so he steadfastly refused, during his eight years of incumbency in the presidential chair, to issue a single religious proclamation.

In being true to his oath of office; in being true to the provisions of the Constitution; in being loyal to the principles of our secular government, Jefferson knew that he would incur the antagonism of the clergy; and in referring to the matter said: "I know it will give great offense to the clergy, but the advocate of religious freedom is to expect neither peace nor forgiveness from them."

In a further elaboration of his act, he laid down this premise, which might well be followed by our present-day executives: "I consider the Government of the United States as interdicted by the Constitution from meddling with religious institutions, their doctrines, disciplines, or exercises. But it is only proposed that I should recommend, not prescribe a day of fasting and praying. That is, I should indirectly assume to the United States an authority over religious exercises, which the constitution has directly precluded them from. Every one must act according to the dictates of his reason and mine, tells me that civil powers alone have been given to the President, and no authority to direct the religious exercises of his constituents."

Not since the days of Jefferson has there been a president with courage enough to live up to the example which he so bravely and so valiantly established.

In keeping with the democratic ideals of the Republic, Jefferson dispensed with all pomp and ceremony with which his two predecessors had surrounded themselves. Jefferson was a Democrat in fact as well as in principle; in practice as well as in theory.

Jefferson was also a Freethinker, in deed as well as in thought; the philosophy of Rationalism ever illuminated his mind. He knew that there was no subject which pertained to the rights, the welfare and the liberty of man which should not be investigated. Age, nor the antiquity of a subject was superior to the interests of mankind. If, after an investigation of a subject it was found to be incompatible with the best interests of life, it felt the force of Jefferson's opposition.

In the volume of Freethought, where can you find the principle set down more clearly than in these words of Jefferson—"Fix reason firmly in her seat, and call to her tribunal every fact, every opinion. Question with boldness even the existence of God; because, if there be one, he must approve the homage of reason rather than of blindfolded fear. Do not be frightened from this inquiry by any fear of its consequences. If it end in a belief that there is no God, you will find incitements to virtue in the comfort and pleasantness you feel in its exercise and in the love of others it will procure for you."

He admonished others to read the Bible as any other book; and if you found recorded therein instances inconsistent with facts, it was the facts which were to be accepted and the authority of the Bible rejected.

Jefferson himself is very explicit upon this phase of his investigation, and he says that Jehovah, the God of the Old Testament was "a being of terrific character, cruel, vindicative, capricious and unjust."

He was equally as emphatic concerning the prophecy of Jesus as found in the New Testament. He said, "The day will come when the mystical generation of Jesus, by the Supreme Being as his father, in the womb of a virgin, will be classified with the fable of the generation of Minerva in the brain of Jupiter."

In a further investigation of the New Testament he found "a groundwork of vulgar ignorance, of things impossible, of superstitions, fanaticism and fabrications."

"If we believe," he continued, "that he (Jesus) really

countenanced the follies, the falsehoods, and the charlatan-isms, which his biographers (Matthew, Mark, Luke and John) father upon him, and admit the misconstructions, interpolations, and theorizations of the father of the early and the fanatics of the latter ages, the conclusion would be irresistible by every sound mind that he was an im-poster."

"Among the sayings and sources imputed to him (Jesus) by his biographers," continues Jefferson, "I find many passages of fine imagination, correct morality, and of the most lovely benevolence; and others again, of so much ignorance, of so much absurdity, so much untruth and imposture, as to pronounce it impossible that such contradictions should have proceeded from the same being. I therefore, separate the gold from the dross, I restore to him the former, and leave the latter to the stupidity of some and the roguery of others of his disciples."

Many a Freethinker owes his emancipation to the read-ing of "Jefferson's Bible," the recorded human events of the Life of the Nazarene as Jefferson interpreted them.

Jefferson was not only convinced of the falsity of the religious dogmas of his day, but militantly struggled to break the grapple hold they had upon the minds of the people, and was happy at every defeat they sustained. In a letter to John Adams, he wrote, "I join you, therefor, in sincere congratulations that the den of priesthood is at length broken up, and that a protestant Popedom is no longer to disgrace the American history and character."

And in response to a letter from John Adams saying, "That this would be the best of all possible worlds if there were no religion in it," Jefferson replied: "If by religion we are to understand sectarian dogmas, in which no two of them agree, then your exclamation on that hypothesis is just, 'that this would be the best of worlds if there were no religion in it.' "

Jefferson was a lover of Voltaire, a correspondent of Volney and an intimate companion of Paine. And we are constrained, in speaking of Jefferson, to mention with the deepest affection, the noble, the generous and the courageous attitude he assumed in sending an American vessel for the safe voyage of Thomas Paine when he sought to leave the shore of France and return to the land of his adoption for which he had labored so heroically.

One of the bravest sentiments ever breathed by man in public life was uttered by Jefferson. He said: "I have never conceived that having been in public life required me to belie my sentiments, or to conceal them. Opinion and the just maintenance of it shall never be a crime in my view, nor bring injury on the individual. I never will, by any word or act, bow to the shrine of intolerance. I never had an opinion in politics or religion which I was afraid to own; a reserve on these subjects might have procured me more esteem from some people, but less from myself."

To that end there was no hesitancy on the part of Jefferson in saying, "I am a Materialist."

In establishing the University of Virginia, Jefferson sought to accomplish in an intellectual sphere for the human race what he and others had accomplished in a political way for mankind. The University of Virginia was to be the counterpart, as an institution of learning, to the Republic.

There were to be no religious tests for pupil or professor, the sciences stood on a par with the classics and mathematics, agriculture and the science of the government were for the first time recognized as subjects worthy of a place in a university curriculum.

In establishing this great institution—the first truly secular college to exist in our land—Jefferson hoped to realize that longed-for and hoped-for day when there would be in reality, some semblance of the Brotherhood of Man.

Jefferson said: "By bringing the sects together, and mixing them with the mass of other students, we shall soften their asperities, liberalize and neutralize their prejudices and make the general religion a religion of peace, reason and morality."

No wonder it was the proud wish of Jefferson that the stone above his grave should not only mention that he was the author of the Declaration of Independence and the Statute of Virginia for Religious Freedom, but also that he was the Father of the University of Virginia.

Despite his invaluable services in behalf of Freedom, despite his unceasing labors for the Republic, despite the everlasting debt the world owes him for his accomplishments, when this great Republican and champion of democratic ideals was elected president of the United States, when the day of his inauguration came to pass, newspapers printed borders of mourning and flags were displayed at half mast as a token of grief because an infidel was to sit in the presidential chair.

What was the reason for these signs of mourning, for

these manifestations of grief? Were they displayed because a calamity was about to befall the Republic?

No. Because a calamity was not impending. On the contrary, during the administration of this infidel, the country more than doubled in size, and by the Louisiana Purchase he laid down the principle of everlasting peace; as a nation we prospered beyond the wildest imagination of the most enthusiastic supporters, and for the first time upon the face of the earth, "life, liberty and the pursuit of happiness" was a reality.

Not because he was dishonest, for he was not; not because he was deficient in administrative ability, for he was not; not because he was morally and intellectually unfitted to be President, for he was the best fitted and best equipped man in the country to guide the destinies of the Republic, but because he was an infidel, and only because he was an infidel, were the signs of mourning and the token of grief displayed by the clergy and their poor duped and deluded supporters on his ascendency as the Chief Magistrate of the Nation.

When the time comes that the American people and the American Government depart from the principles of Jefferson, then it will be time for us as a token of grief to border our papers with the black band of mourning and lower the American flag to half mast, aye, with tears in our eyes, and our frames shaking with emotion, as though we are burying a loved one, we can pull down the American flag and with all the solemnity which this emblem deserves, tenderly and silently fold it away, that the future may behold the symbol of Freedom, recount its glories, and mourn the death of the Star Spangled Banner.

When we depart from the principles of Jefferson, our Republic will have ceased to exist.

We cannot honor Thomas Jefferson more, we cannot more fittingly pay tribute to the memory of this great Statesman, Libertarian and Freethinker, than by living up to those high principles which he so nobly and so courageously wrote into the Declaration of Independence.

FRANKLIN
THE FREETHINKER

by

Joseph Lewis

Author of "The Tyranny of God," "The Bible Unmasked,"
"Lincoln, the Freethinker," "Burbank, the Infidel," "Jefferson, the Freethinker," "Atheism," "Voltaire, the Incomparable Infidel," "The Bible and the Public Schools," "Shall Children Receive Religious Instruction?" "Mexico and the Church," "Spain: Land Blighted by Religion," etc.

THE FREETHOUGHT PRESS ASSOCIATION, INC.

317 EAST 34th STREET, NEW YORK, N. Y.

FRANKLIN, THE FREETHINKER *

We meet to-night to celebrate the memory of one of the most illustrious men of the human race, and one of the grandest benefactors of mankind who ever "touched this bank and shoal of time."

No character in all the world was as many-sided as this great genius who did so much for the progress and development of the race, and who played so major a part in the establishment of our Republic.

The energies of this patriot, philosopher, inventor, discoverer, scientist and humanitarian knew no bounds, and he loved life not for itself alone, but for the usefulness he could render mankind through living. Hardly a spot on the face of the earth has not been benefited for his having lived.

This all-embracing genius was not divinely conceived, nor miraculously born. His parentage is authentically recorded, and as an infant he was not found in the bulrushes; and yet, if there ever was a "Moses," the symbol of a divine lawgiver with a message from the God of the Universe (if there be one), his name was Benjamin Franklin!

His code of morals is far superior to the broken tablets of Sinai. And despite the fact that Benjamin Franklin was a child of "God-fearing" parents, he was born an infidel, a heretic and a skeptic. *He was born on Sunday!* The first word uttered was a cry of blasphemy, a thundering defiance to Jehovah, and a challenge to the superstitious of his day. For in Franklin's day to be born on Sunday meant to have been *conceived* on Sunday, and no such desecration should be

* Address delivered January 17, 1925 by Joseph Lewis at the banquet of the Freethinkers' Society of New York, at the Hotel Astor, New York City.—Also over Radio Station WGBS.

made of the Sabbath, which belonged wholly and exclusively to the Lord. The Lord's Day Alliance of that time should have been more vigilant in the day of Franklin's parents.

He was the youngest son of the youngest son for five generations, and you can easily perceive with what precision was this man sent to defy the God of his day.

Although given a strict religious training in his childhood, with much thought devoted to preparing him for the ministry, fortunately we find Franklin in his early manhood frequenting a club of Freethinkers. Once emancipated from the narrowness and bigotry of religious dogma, his heart and mind were free for the love of mankind.

The great fault with the human race is not lack of love, but *misdirected* love. Nearly all the wealth, energy, and intellect of the world have been squandered upon religion. So much love was given to "God" that there was none left for the human family. To fear God and appease his anger by worshipping him was believed to be the highest duty of man in those days.

Franklin's endeavors were not to lessen that love which springs eternal in the human heart, but to direct it from the sky to the earth. Were humanity loved with but half the zeal that has been bestowed upon "The Prince of the Power of the Air," the human family would not be in its present desperate plight. Hatred, bigotry and prejudice would long since have vanished from the human mind. The problems of disease, dissension and war would have long since been solved. Happiness would now be reigning upon the earth, and injustice would be as rare as is justice to-day. The question of buttoning the collar in front or behind would be material fit only for the comic sheet.

Since Sunday was the day Franklin chose for his appearance upon earth, he very early in life made it his business to devote that day to reading and writing and the cultivation of his intellect. Sundays, he said, were too precious to be wasted on prayer meetings when they could be used for mental culture. Was a fairer exchange ever made? And yet Franklin was not without his reason for not attending Sunday services of the church. Franklin did not do things without a reason, and a good and sufficient reason at that; and so he gives us his reasons for not attending church services.

"The Discourses of the preachers," he said, "were chiefly arguments of explanation of the peculiar doctrines of their sects," and these doctrines he found to be "dry, uninteresting, and unedifying; not a single moral principle was inculcated or enforced." In fact, he said: "the aim seemed to be rather to make us good Presbyterians [that was the creed of his parents] than good citizens."

Franklin believed in good works rather than in worship. "Revealed religion," he said, "had no weight with me"; and here he makes the vital distinction between religion and morals, when he said "truth, sincerity, and integrity in dealings between man and man are of the utmost importance to the felicity of life." The church is concerned with making good adherents to the creed, and not in making good citizens. Morality is concerned with good citizenship.

Franklin states further, that religion does not tend to inspire, promote, or confirm morality, but serves principally to divide us and make us unfriendly to one another. "Serving God," says Poor Richard, "is doing good to man, but praying is thought an easier serving, and therefore most generally chosen."

The charge that unbelief is without an incentive to good actions is refuted by Franklin himself. When the preacher Whitefield visited America, he found himself without lodging, and the good Franklin offered him the hospitality of his home.

Referring to Whitefield's acceptance, Franklin writes: "He replied that, if I made that offer for Christ's sake, I should not miss a reward. And I returned, *'Don't let me be mistaken; it was not for Christ's sake, but for your sake.'*"

The preacher Whitefield often prayed for his host's conversion, but "never," said Franklin, "had the satisfaction of believing that his prayers were heard."

Morality was always the important thing to Franklin's mind and anything that tended to promote morality received his hearty support. Perhaps it was for this reason that he so often criticized religion.

Although Franklin avoided churchgoing, there were times when he attended church, and his experiences are well worth noting. After following a crowd of people on a Sunday morning, he was led into the great meeting house of the Quakers. "There," he said, "I sat down among them, and, looking around awhile and hearing nothing said, being very drowsy through labor and want of rest the preceding night, *I fell asleep,* and continued so till the meeting broke up, when one was kind enough to arouse me. This was, therefore, the first house I was in, or slept in, in Philadelphia."

No one can object to the church being put to such a use; and were all churches converted into lodging houses, their benefit to society would be increased manyfold.

On another occasion, Franklin was attracted to church by a young preacher named Hamphill, whose sermons, Franklin said, we not of the dogmatic kind, but "inculcated strongly the practice of virtue or good works." The older clergymen of that time were vociferous in their denunciation of the strange young preacher, and branded his appearance as a "dreadful plot laid by Satan to root Christianity out of the world," asserting that his eloquence attracted only "Free-thinkers, Deists, and nothings." Needless to say clergymen were not more liberal then than they are now, and the young preacher was tried for heresy and convicted. It is interesting to note that the only clergyman who commanded the attention of Franklin was so liberal in his views that he was put out of the Church.

Church disputes were prevalent in Franklin's day just as they are in our time, and will continue to be until the church abandons its false premise. On this point Franklin said: "Each party abuses the other; the profane and the infidel believe both sides, and enjoy the fray; the reputation of religion in general suffers and its enemies are ready to say, not what was said in primitive times, 'Behold how these Christians love one another,' but 'Mark how these Christians hate one another!' Indeed, when religious people quarrel about religion, or hungry people quarrel about victuals, it looks as if they had not much of either among them."

Franklin thought that "original sin" was a detestable doctrine, and his idea of the Sabbath may be summarized by his reference to his partner, a Mr. Keimer: "Keimer wore his beard long, because Moses has somewhere said, 'Thou shalt not mar the corners of thy beard.' He likewise observed the Sabbath; and these were with him two very essential points. *I disliked them both.*"

And when Franklin was in Paris this observation struck him very forcibly, and in a letter to a friend he wrote: "When I traveled in Flanders I thought of your excessively strict observation of Sunday, and that a man could hardly travel on that day among you upon his lawful occasions without hazard of punishment, while where I was everyone traveled, if he pleased, or diverted himself in any other way, and in the afternoon both high and low went to the play or the opera, where there was plenty of singing, fiddling, and dancing. I looked around for God's judgments, but saw no sign of them. The cities were built and full of inhabitants, the market filled with plenty, the people well favored and well clothed, the fields well tilled, the cattle fat and strong, the fences, houses and windows all in repair, and no 'old tenor' anywhere in the country; which would make one almost suspect that the Deity was not so angry at that offense as a New England justice."

These words of Franklin should be engraved upon fine parchment, suitably framed, and presented to the Lord's Day Alliance.

Franklin's complete emancipation from the superstitions of his day came about when, as he said, "Some volumes against Deism fell into my hands. They were said to be the substance of sermons preached at Boyle's lecture. It happened that they produced on me an effect the opposite of what was intended by the writer; for the arguments of the Deists, which were cited in order to be refuted, appealed to me much more forcibly than the refutation itself. In a word I soon became a thorough Deist." The word "Deist" of Franklin's day has its exact counterpart in the word "Freethinker" to-day. And how many thousands of our leading men and women have been emancipated as a result of theologians quoting Free-thought arguments in an endeavor to answer them?

We cannot overlook the influence exercised upon Franklin's mind by his association with that little club of Freethinkers with which he came in contact early in life. The discussions he heard there opened his mind to see both sides of a controversy; they taught him to use reason as his guide.

A little more than a hundred years later, another band of Freethinkers were again to give to the world an invaluable contribution when it freed the mind of Abraham Lincoln from the supersitions of religion and stirred him to the needs and want of humanity. And perhaps in our own band of Freethinkers there is a Franklin or a Lincoln in the making.

Although not yet eighteen years of age, says one of his biographers, Franklin began to write vigorous attacks against religion. And when the opportunity presented itself to assist his brother in publishing a paper called the *New England Courant,* the pen that was destined to be read and admired the world over poured its satire upon the miserable and degrading superstitions of Puritanism. Although his brother was jailed for the blasphemies, for which no doubt Benjamin was responsible, Franklin continued with his assaults upon the stupidities of his time.

In humor, Franklin found one of his most effective weapons against religion. And oh, how deadly is humor to religion! Joy is a child of Satan. His most successful hoax was the composition of a satire of the fifty-first chapter of Genesis. In the language of the Bible he wrote out a parable against persecution, and committed it to memory. Then, whenever the question of religion was discussed, he would very solemnly open the Bible and seemingly begin to read—to the mystification and ultimate confusion of his opponents.

Piqued and stung by the constant lashing and ridicule heaped upon them by this unusual young man, the clergy sought protection from further attacks.

No less a personage than Cotton Mather was prompted to pay this tribute to Franklin's courage and daring: The *New*

England Courant, he declared, was "full-freighted with nonsense, unmanliness, raillery, profaneness, immorality, arrogance, calumnies, lies, contradictions, and what not, all tending to quarrels and division and to debauch and corrupt the minds and manners of New England.

Coming from a man of the mentality of Cotton Mather, I consider this the greatest tribute that was ever paid to Franklin. And yet I doubt very much whether some of the clergymen of to-day have advanced intellectually very much further than this Puritan divine.

To prove the charges against this blasphemous paper and bring about its suppression, Increase Mather quotes this statement from its pages:

"If ministers of God approve of a thing, it is a sign it is of the devil; which is a hard thing to be related."

Franklin may have written this merely as a piece of satire, but many a true word is spoken in jest.

Even Harvard College was not free from Franklin's attacks. For he wrote that most of the graduates, whom he characterized as stupid, went into the Church which he described as a temple of Ambition and Fraud, controlled by money.

This virile paper was finally suppressed, "because it mocked religion, brought the Holy Scriptures into contempt and profanely abused the faithful ministers of God."

Franklin was a prophet of far more accuracy than the Apostles of Doom of his day, and although he was *not* a divinely appointed representative of God, who can deny he did not possess supernatural prophetic powers in his prediction:

"Of the Fruits of the Earth."

"I find this will be a plentiful year of all manner of good things, to those who have enough; but the Orange Trees in Greenland will go near to fare the worse for the Cold. As for Oats, they'll be a great Help to Horses."

Much awe and reverence are inspired by the so-called miracle of Christ and Peter walking upon the water; but it is not generally known that Franklin was capable of *sleeping* upon the water. He records this miraculous performance himself in the following note:

"I went at noon in the Martin salt-water bath, and, floating on my back, fell asleep, and slept near an hour by my watch without sinking or turning! a thing I never did before and should have hardly thought possible. Water is the easiest bed that can be."

Persecution did not deter Franklin from his criticism of the Bible nor of religion in general. In an essay on "Toleration" note with what force he states the truth:

"If we look back into history for the character of the present sects of Christianity, we shall find that few have not in their turn been persecutors, and complainers of persecution. The primitive Christians thought persecution extremely wrong in the Pagans, but practiced it on one another. The first Protestants of the Church of England blamed persecution in the Romish Church, but practiced it upon the Puritans. These found it wrong in Bishops, but fell into the same practice themselves in England and America."

All of which merely emphasizes the fact that Religious Liberty is safe only in the hands of the Freethinker, whose philosophy of freedom of thought is expressed by Thomas Paine in the words, "He who would make his own liberty secure, must guard even his enemy from oppression." Religious sects differ about interpretation; the minority use the arguments of liberalism to justify their existence; but history proves, as Franklin so pungently puts it, that when minorities become the majorities and possess the power, dogmatism overshadows the principles of Liberty which permitted their existence, and they in turn become the persecutors of others and are as tyrannical with their powers as those who previously endeavored to force them to conformity.

The philosophy of Freethought is the principle of the open mind. Difference of opinion and the unbound avenue of investigation are essential to its existence. It gives the same right to change an opinion as to accept one, and respects the honest conclusions of others. Is it any wonder, then, that the

Freethinker Franklin could travel from one country to another and be respected by all the differing sects? He looked with understanding and sympathy upon them all.

Franklin knew the importance of placing all religions upon the same basis, and when he laid down this premise it was one of the soundest pieces of political advice that this great statesman gave to the world in his vast volume of political philosophy.

He said: *"When a religion is good, I conceive it will support itself; and when it does not support itself, and God does not take care to support it, so that its professors are obliged to call for help of the civil powers, 'tis a sign, I apprehend, of its being a bad one."*

If the exemption of church property continues to be granted in this country, a problem of no mean dimensions will have to be faced before many years have passed. Franklin never gave a better warning nor sounder advice than when he made that statement.

"To exempt the church from taxation," says Ingersoll, "is to pay part of the priest's salary."

Let us resolve now, in the name and memory of the great Franklin, to wage a relentless war upon this unjust taxation of the people. Let us inscribe on our banner: "Equal rights for all, special privileges to none."

The fame of Franklin, having spread far and wide for the blessings his genius had brought to the people, prompted many communities to do honor to his name. One particular community in the State of Massachusetts decided to name their town after him. And, as they also wished to build a steeple to their church, they asked him to make a contribution toward the bell. In a letter to Richard Price, of England, a well-known infidel of that time, Franklin thus sets forth his views:

"My nephew, Mr. Williams, will have the honor of delivering you this line. It is to request from you a list of books, to the value of twenty-five pounds, such as are most proper to inculcate sound religion and good government. A town in the State of Massachusetts having done me the honor of naming itself after me, and proposing to build a steeple to their meeting house if I would give them a bell, I have advised the sparing themselves the expense of a steeple, for the present, and that they would accept the books instead of a bell, sense being preferred to sound."

And remember that Dr. Price, the infidel, was the one whom Franklin instructed to select the books that would be most conducive to "sound religion and good government."

On another occasion, while traveling to Europe with his son, his ship encountered a storm at sea, and was saved from shipwreck through the fortunate existence of a lighthouse. In writing to his wife of this experience, Franklin said: "If I were a Catholic, on my arrival home I would ask subscriptions to build a church, but being an unbeliever, will raise the money to build a lighthouse instead."

While speaking of England and Franklin's association with that country, I must not forget to mention that while there Franklin was seen regularly at a coffee house, the haven of Freethinkers.

It was at this coffee house that he met a young man who was desirous of making his acquaintance—a young man whose name was Thomas Paine. And if Franklin did nothing else to entitle him to the everlasting gratitude of the American people, the letter of introduction which he gave Paine, with the advice that he come to the American shores to make his home, would be sufficient.

And in discussing Thomas Paine and the religious convictions of Benjamin Franklin I would be remiss in my duty if I failed to make mention of the fraud perpetrated upon the honored names of both of these illustrious men.

It is claimed by some religious zealots, that before publishing his immortal *Age of Reason* Paine showed the manuscript to Franklin to get his opinion of it. And Franklin is said to have written Paine a rather lengthy letter, in which he advised him against the publication of the book. The letter was supposed to have been found among the effects of Franklin *after* his death and had been captioned, "Don't Unchain the Tiger." The sense of the letter is, that if people are so bad with religion they will be worse without it.

Since it is frequently necessary to refute the lies that have so often been woven around our great men, in order to get a true estimate of them, it is needful to expose this falsehood that a true conception of Franklin and Paine may be made plain to all, and at the same time expose the mendacity and the desperate ends to which the religious forces will go to vilify the name of one and falsify the words of another in order to accomplish their vicious ends.

I doubt that Franklin ever wrote that letter, or, if he did, that it was intended for Paine. The letter is addressed to no one, and superscribed by no one. And does anyone believe that if Franklin really wrote that letter he would not have signed it? Franklin was accused of many things by the enemies of his day, but cowardice was not one of them. And how could Franklin condemn in another the very things he had himself been doing? Did not Franklin attack religion at every opportunity? And are not the sentiments contained in the *Age of Reason* identical with the thoughts expressed by Franklin?

Could a more vicious piece of propaganda be circulated to discredit two of the greatest men of America just because they were unorthodox in religion, disbelievers in the inspiration of the Bible, and doubters of the divinity of Christ?

But another important point concerning this letter, and perhaps the most important of all, is this: Franklin is supposed to have written this letter in 1786. Paine did not write the *Age of Reason* until 1793, when he was confined in the Luxembourg prison in Paris. Franklin died in 1790, three years before the *Age of Reason* was published! Moreover, Paine specifically states that "I follow the rule I began with Common Sense, that is, to consult nobody, nor let anybody see what I write till it appears publicly." With these facts before us how is it possible that this letter, supposedly written by Franklin, referred to the *Age of Reason?*

This letter that Franklin is supposed to have written to Paine brings to mind the charge made concerning Ingersoll and his profligate son.

An all too pious clergyman had stated that Ingersoll's son, bred in a home of Infidelity, had gone insane, and had died in an insane asylum; to which Ingersoll replied; "My son was not a profligate; he was never insane, he did not die in an asylum; in fact, I never had a son."

And then again, how can such a letter be representative of Franklin's convictions, when at the age of eighty, but three years before his death, he wrote to a correspondent in England, in which he asks to be remembered "affectionately to good Dr. Price and the honest heretic, Dr. Priestly," and continues:

"I do not call him honest by way of distinction, for I think all the heretics I have known have been virtuous men. They have the virtue of fortitude, or they would not venture to own their heresy; and they cannot afford to be deficient in any of their virtues, as that would give advantage to their enemies; and they have not, like orthodox sinners, such a number of friends to excuse or justify them. Do not, however, mistake me. It is not, my good friends, to heresy that I impute his honesty. On the contrary, it is his honesty that has brought upon his head the character of a heretic."

Few of us to-day can fully realize the mental night that darkened the world in Franklin's time. Witchcraft was everywhere dominant. Every conceivable superstition held sway over the minds of the people. The most horrible crimes were committed in the name of religion. Cotton and Increase Mather were the intellects who ruled. And although the great souls who lived before Franklin had broken to some degree the tyrannical power of priest and king, and here and there the monsters of religion had been driven from the face of the earth, the winds, the rain, the storm, the sunshine and the seasons were still believed to be the caprices of God. And even though you were not burned at the stake for disbelieving the inspiration of the Bible, the wrath of God would yet fall upon you at Judgment Day. The cringing mass was awed into submission by warnings from above. Was not thunder the voice of God: and did not lightning reveal his anger and strike many dead?

But in 1752, on the banks of the Schuylkill River, came one of the most significant triumphs for the liberation of man. Benjamin Franklin, through his successful experiment with the kite, discovered the true nature of electricity, tore the mask from the face of Jehovah, and freed the heavens of a hideous monster.

The thunderbolt was no longer the manifestation of God's anger, nor the lightning of his wrath. The mind of man was completely emancipated from the fear of God.

It is difficult to realize the complete revolution this discovery made upon the human race, or how far it was responsible for the triumphs of the nineteenth century. With it Franklin's fame, already world-wide, was intensified into universal approbation.

The only dissenting voice was that of the clergy. They feared with their whole being, and rightly, too, the consequences of his achievement,—the lightning rod. They roundly termed it the "heretical rod" and refused to desecrate their churches with it, although as a consequence God particularly singled them out for destruction. Prayer, supplication and the ringing of bells were the methods they employed to forestall the lightning or to calm the rising flood.

The clergy of that day, not unlike some to-day, could not reconcile their calling with the impious work of an "arch infidel." There has always been hesitancy in accepting the achievements of the leaders and pioneers of progress, and always because it was in conflict with "God's word."

History is but a continuous narrative of the steps of progress, each one of which the Church has bitterly contested.

Franklin's "Heretical Rod" has been a mighty instrument for the liberation and progress of man. It has released us from the terror of the Unknown, and the debt the world owes this infidel is greater than it can pay.

After a life so full of good works, so resplendent with achievements, so crowded with accomplishments, and so marked with unselfishness, this grand man, grander than all the saints, honored the world over and loved by his countrymen as their father, "shuffled off his mortal coil"; and, although he wrote an epitaph for his tomb, what more appropriate and fitting could be said of this great Freethinker than those words of Shakespeare:

> "The elements were
> So mixed in him that Nature might stand up
> And say to all the world 'This was a man.'"

BURBANK—
THE INFIDEL

by

Joseph Lewis

Author of "The Tyranny of God," "The Bible Unmasked,"
"Lincoln, the Freethinker," "Jefferson, the Freethinker,"
"Atheism," "Franklin, the Freethinker," "Voltaire, the In-
comparable Infidel," "The Bible and the Public Schools,"
"Shall Children Receive Religious Instruction?" "Mexico and
the Church," "Spain: Land Blighted by Religion," etc.

THE FREETHOUGHT PRESS ASSOCIATION, INC.

317 EAST 34th STREET, NEW YORK, N. Y.

Dedicated
With Deep Affection
to

THOMAS A. EDISON

Genius, Inventor, Humanitarian
and World's Greatest Benefactor

LUTHER BURBANK

By Edith Daley

The gentlest man in all the world is dead—
So understanding in his thought of her
That Nature made him her Interpreter,
And crowned him with the sun about his head;
Crowned him with sun, and gave him Love instead
Of human greed; such Love that eyes now blur
With tears, while memory's lavender and myrrh
Breathe in the blossom-pall upon his bed.
He sleeps as gently as he lived; and high
Among the trees, and underneath where blow
The April buds, the green earth seems to know
And grieve—and hush—and softly say:
"Good-bye!"
And all who love him, where the blossoms bend,
Lean low to hear all Nature whisper: "Friend!"

From the Laboratory
of
Thomas A. Edison.

Orange, N.J.

January
twenty-fifth
1930

Mr. Joseph Lewis,
250 West 54th St.,
New York City.

My dear Mr. Lewis:

It was a cause of much regret to me that I found it
impossible to carry out my part of your
programme by planting a tree in Central Park
in memory of my greatly esteemed friend,
Luther Burbank.

It was indeed a most fitting manner of perpetuating
the memory of one whose every thought and
heart-thob had their inspiration in the
glorious beauties of Nature. Being a sincere
admirer of this supremely simple but wonderful
man and his achievments, I regarded it as a
great privilege to have spent some little time
with Mr. Burbank at his home in Santa Rosa a
few years ago.

Despite his unaffected bearing and simplicity of manner
one could not help but feel that here was a
Master in his own chosen field, and thus I found
him.

I am rejoiced that he accepted me as a friend.

Yours very truly,

Thos A Edison.

Ediphoned-C

BURBANK THE INFIDEL

On April 11, Luther Burbank died.

His death was not only a bereavement to his family and friends, but the entire country, aye, the whole civilized world mourned his passing.

The world mourned because a man had died who had brought happiness to the human race; had added to the sum total of knowledge, and had made the world better for his having lived.

Luther Burbank was a rare spirit, a tender soul. He was a noble son of the earth and his death was an irreparable loss to mankind.

We honor Luther Burbank today not only for his independence of thought, although that alone would entitle him to our homage, but also because of his achievements as a scientist and his accomplishments in the realm of Nature.

Stone and marble do not seem to be fit attributes for this lover of Nature and so we plant a tree to his memory. It symbolizes more appropriately his life and work.

Flowers and plants and trees were his intimates and formed part of his family.

He loved them as we love human beings and they became as much a part of his life and existence as if he were born one of them. This close intimacy gave him a familiarity possessed by no other man. He learned the secrets of the plants and spoke the language of the flowers. So remarkably intimate was he with life in the flower kingdom that he became known as "The Wizard of Plant Life."

He moved in a mysterious way among them his wonders to perform. He nurtured a flower as we do a child and it seemed to love him for it. A broken branch of a tree touched him to pity, and the wanton destruction of flowers

Address delivered on May 22, 1927, in Central Park, New York City, at the Tree-Planting Memorial Exercises, conducted by the Freethinkers of America, in honor of Luther Burbank, who was a member and First Honorary Vice-President.

was a grievous hurt to him. He cured sick flowers, brought beauty to ugly ones and sweet odors to all.

From early life he manifested a kinship with them and often when provoked by pain to tears his mother would place a flower in his hands and a smile would appear on his tear-stained cheeks. He took the rough and uncouth of plant life and brought beauty and charm to them by the magic of his touch. Flowers seemed to obey him like good children a kind parent. No man had greater love for them. And no man was more tenderly revered by them.

Burbank also loved children, his country and mankind. His life was one continuous romance. He lived like a man forever falling in love with his wife and child and family. What a glorious feeling to be in love and happy and live!

He gave as freely of his work as flowers their perfume. He made the earth a better, brighter, and more beautiful place than he found it, and the world is healthier and happier for his having lived. More cannot be said of any man. Even a god would be proud of such a record.

It is impossible at this time to comprehend the immensity of Burbank's work, and the benefits his researches and experimentations have brought to mankind.

It is even impossible to calculate the value in health and the amount of enjoyment his creations of fruits, flowers and vegetables have been even to this generation.

Millions are enjoying the fruits of his labors without the slightest knowledge of their benefactor.

Laws of selection, variation and heredity which he discovered and applied are in themselves invaluable instruments of knowledge with which to accomplish among human beings what he so marvelously achieved with plants.

Burbank's work is not done, it has really just begun. His death ended his own labors but placed a tremendous responsibility upon the living. Thousands are now required to do the work that he alone performed.

On March 7, 1849, Luther Burbank was born.

Twenty-six years later he entered Santa Rosa, California, the little town which he made his home and which he has since immortalized. He lies buried there beneath a tree he planted.

It is said that he came to this little town with but ten dollars, ten potatoes and a few choice books.

Three authors of these books inspired him in his life's work. They were, Henry Thomas Thoreau, Charles Robert

Darwin, whom he loved to call "Master," and Alexander Von Humboldt, who imbued him with the spirit of the importance and worth of his work.

These three men inspired him with a burning desire to accomplish, a confidence that only one genius can impart to another, and with an idealism known only to the few heroic men and women who have been mankind's benefactors.

And it is most fitting for us to plant this tree as a memorial to Burbank that it may grow and spread its verdant leaves as a shade over the magnificent head of this "Columbus of Science."

His material equipment was indeed poor, his body was not overstrong, and his heart was broken. He had been unsuccessful in love. He tried to mend his broken heart by lavishing his love upon his beautiful garden and upon the flowers he loved as his children. And what an abundance of love he had, and with what abandonment he lavished it!

He added strength to his body by living close to Nature, and following the advice of Mother Earth.

Enraptured in his work he began his labors of more than a half of a century.

Although Burbank came to Santa Rosa unknown and in poverty, the world made a beaten path to his door. The celebrated and the famous the world over came to pay homage to this "Gardener touched with genius."

By the fruits of his labor he gave incalculable wealth to others.

Do not let it be said, however, that Burbank's accomplishments were the result of a magic wand. He labored assiduously and found competition most keen.

There may be room always at the top, but there is always a crowd that must be pushed aside in the middle of the road so as to clear the passage for the ascent.

Burbank found many botanists, and horticulturists, and plain gardeners who were doing things a bit above the ordinary, and he realized early in life that if he was to distinguish himself he must do something that had not been done before.

The obstacles that he found in his path did not prove to be millstones around his neck, but rather milestones on his road to fame.

Each difficulty proved a new experience, and a new experience to Burbank meant more knowledge with which to work. He built his knowledge upon experience and experiments.

He had a keenness of perception not surpassed by any man. He watched for the slightest variation to wrest a secret from Nature. Experience is the only knowledge we possess and is the basis for the development of our mind. In Burbank's experiment with the cactus he discovered how intelligence is gradually formed through experience and manifests itself through what we call instinct.

As with Edison, perspiration was the predominant part of his inspiration. No task was too arduous for him and he permitted no obstacle to stand in his way. He knew the ends he wished to accomplish and determinedly set about his work.

He did not always work from appearances. Appearances, he found, were as deceiving in flowers as in human beings, and he often went back many generations to correct a fault.

A changed environment invariably changed the character of the flower, but to eradicate a deep-seated fault it was sometimes necessary to operate upon the roots.

Once he learned the secrets of Nature, once he learned to talk to Nature in her own language, Burbank became proficient in conversation. A more brilliant conversationalist the plants have never known. Once on speaking terms with Nature he established a friendship never to be broken. His loyalty never wavered.

He was also an apt pupil. He studied her alphabet, mastered her grammer, punctuation and rhetoric and wrote many pages in the book of Life which only a few are privileged to do.

"I took Nature's mind and added it to my own," said Burbank, "and by so doing bridged centuries of time in adding sweetness and charm and color to Nature's products."

He married beauty and strength and sweetness to produce the Ideal.

He took Nature by the hand, so ot speak, and led her into paths of beauty that she had not dreamed existed. With his help he made Nature excel herself and sit and marvel at her wonders.

Burbank did not claim occult powers. He did not pose with a halo around his head. He did not boast that he was "divinely inspired." He performed no miracles, although he accomplished marvels.

He gladly, freely and generously gave his knowledge to others. He was an intellectual spendthrift "What I have learned, you may learn," are his words.

His soul was the heart of a true scientist.

Where did Burbank learn the great truths that he applied so effectively and so ardently wanted man to follow? Why was he so sure that they would be as successful in the human realm as they were in the plant kingdom?

Surely his own academic education was not sufficient to give him this grasp of Nature, nor was his technical training sufficient to enable him to perform his wonders.

His early schooling was the barest rudiments that the little Red School House had to offer.

The secret of his marvelous intellect and his ability to apply the knowledge he acquired are told in his own words.

He received a scholarship which anyone with a desire for knowledge may secure also. He said: "My school has been the University of Nature. I matriculated in the College of Horticulture, Department of Market Gardening, but I finished that course in short time and entered the laboratory where Nature teaches Plant Breeding. I cannot say that I graduated from that branch of the Institution even yet—there is so much to learn! But in the years that I have been a student I have spread out considerably and taken something pretty nearly of every course my Alma Mater offers except Football and Public Speaking. I was not taught everything, but was taught the fundamentals behind everything!"

In the University of Nature, Burbank not only learned about plants and flowers and trees and vegetables, but also about rocks and soil and mountains and rivers, about birds and fish and horses and cows and dogs and men.

He was told by the great Humboldt that "the Universe was governed by law," and in the University of Nature, Burbank verified this great truth!

Burbank wanted others to enter the University from which he was graduated with such high honors and in these words differentiated it from any other college in existence.

"The great difference between my favorite University and the schools men build is that the ambitious and the interested student can enroll for life and take every course offered, and each fact he adds to his store, and semester of work he does, fits him precisely and definitely for the next subject ahead without any loss of motion and without a line that is superfluous to him."

The University of Nature might well be proud of the distinguished career of her pupil and above the portals of her entrance should be inscribed these words of his.

"Nature is not personal. She is the compound of all these processes which move through the universe to effect the results we know as Life and of all the ordinances which govern that universe and that make Life continuous. She is no more the Hebrew's Jehovah than she is the Physicist's Force; she is as much Providence as she is Electricity; she is not the Great Pattern any more than she is the Blind Chance."

A great artist was once asked by a lady admirer what he mixed his paints with to get such marvelous results, and he answered: "With brains, madam." Burbank's brain bore the same relation to flowers as did the artist's to his paints.

With an almost uncanny touch the artist can, with a daub of paint, change the perspective of his picture; and so sensitive was Burbank to the pulse of the flower, that he could, with the slightest touch, make it perform wonders for him.

In his own words he defines this unusual characteristic. "It was with this instinct for selection that I was gifted. It was born in me, and I educated and gave it experience, and have always kept myself attuned to it. I have particularly sensitive nerves—that accounts partly for my unusual success in selecting, as between two apparently identical plants and flowers or trees and fruits. I have always been sensitive to odors, so that I could detect them, pleasant or disagreeable, when they were so slight that no one about me was conscious of them."

Burbank never grew old in mind or body. He was as ready to accept a new truth as to discard a wrong impression.

This attitude of mind is the first requisite of knowledge. It is the first principle of an alert intellect.

And these words of Burbank should become an axiom in our language:

"Intolerance is a closed mind. Bigotry is an exaltation of authorities. Narrowness is ignorance unwilling to be taught."

That he did not consider the Bible a divine revelation can be attested by these words of advice:

"Let us read the Bible without the ill-fitting colored spectacles of theology, just as we read other books, using our own judgment and reason, listening to the voice within, not to the noisy babel without. Most of us possess discriminating reasoning powers. Can we use them or must we be fed by others like babes?"

No dogmatism hampered Burbank. No theology prevented him from peering into the unknown. He never permitted himself to become set in his opinions.

"Folks wonder how I keep so young!" he said. "I am almost seventy-seven and still can go over a gate or run a foot race or kick the chandelier. That is because my body is no older than my mind, and my mind is adolescent. It has never grown up. It never will, I hope. I am as inquisitive as I was at eight."

To those who ask us "what will you give us in exchange" when we free them from their superstitious religion, how pertinent and precious are these words of Burbank. I wish they could be impressed upon the mind of every living person. "I have seen myself," he says, "lose intolerance, narrowness, bigotry, complacence, pride and a whole bushel-basket of other intellectual vices through my contact with Nature and with men. And when you take weeds out of a garden it gives you room to grow flowers. So, everytime I lost a little self-satisfaction, or arrogance, I could plant some broadness or love of my own in its place, and after a while the garden of my mind began to bloom and be fragrant and I found myself better equipped for my work and more useful to others as a consequence."

"I have learned from Nature that dependence on unnatural beliefs weakens us in the struggle and shortens our breath for the race," said Burbank, and in the twilight of life, when he knew that the end was approaching, he said that "the time had come for honest men to denounce false teachers and attack false gods" and with a courage characteristic of this great and grand man he proclaimed to the world that he was an infidel!

When Burbank made this declaration, the theological hyenas were ready to tear the flesh from his body. They maligned and vilified him, and tried to inter the good that he did with his bones.

When he made that statement, however, he classed himself with Franklin, Jefferson, Paine, Lincoln and Ingersoll.

Burbank refused to accept the dogma and religion of his time because he knew that they were poisoning the brain and mentality of man. They were paralyzing the intellect. He looked upon them as weeds that must of necessity be rooted out before man could think freely and act properly upon the problems of life.

Because of his fame, and despite his open declaration, the religious world is making an attempt to claim him as one of their members. What hypocrisy!

Luther Burbank was not religious!

His name cannot be mentioned in the same breath with that impulse, with that conviction which produces religious mania, religious strife, religious hatred and religious prejudice.

Religious love is clannish.

Christian loves Christian.

Jew loves Jew.

Luther Burbank loved everybody. He said: "I love everything. I love humanity. I love flowers. I love children. I love my dog."

Luther Burbank was not religious—he was too human for that.

He was a humanitarian, a lover of mankind.

A religious person loves his God. He loves his God so vehemently that he has no love left for man.

Burbank hated the idea of an all-powerful God and said: "The idea that a good God would send people to a burning hell is utterly damnable to me. The ravings of insanity! Superstition gone to seed! I don't want to have anything to do with such a God."

And in a letter from him, shortly before he died, in response to my request for a statement indicative of his belief, he wrote, "This should be enough for one who lives for truth and service to his fellow passengers on the way. No avenging Jewish God, no satanic devil, no fiery hell is of any interest to me."

A religious man attends church, observes feast days and fast days. He takes part in religious ceremonies and pays the priest to pray for him.

"Prayer," says Burbank, "may be elevating if combined with work, and they who labor with head, hands or feet have faith and are generally quite sure of an immediate and favorable reply."

To pray for that which you have not labored for is the most selfish impulse in life.

A religious man is one who has sold his brain, and who has mortgaged his intellect. He believes in a Heaven and in a Hell.

Burbank asked for no Heaven because he knew that it did not exist, and he feared no Hell because he knew that there was none.

No, Luther Burbank was not a religious man. He was a good man. He was a grand man—one of the grandest that ever lived on this earth.

Moses, and Jesus and Torquemada were religious. So were

John Calvin and John Knox and John Wesley and Martin Luther and Cotton Mather. The Pope is religious.

Hypatia and Bruno and Galileo were infidels. So were Ernest Haeckel and Herbert Spencer and Charles P. Steinmetz and Voltaire and Thomas Paine and John Burroughs and Mark Twain. Clarence Darrow was an infidel.

Luther Burbank is dead.

His lips were sealed in death with the same conviction that was his philosophy while he lived.

And now that he is gone we seek to honor his memory with the fullness of our love.

We have come not to honor a soldier or a statesman. No bugle is to sound taps for his military triumphs. We are honoring a simple, lovable man.

One who was a saver of life, a benefactor, a creator of joy, a dispenser of happiness.

One who was not revengeful or vindictive.

One who would rather have made a mistake on the side of mercy than to have a single human being suffer because of his mistake.

Those who were privileged to know Luther Burbank have lost a friend. Our country has lost one of her chosen sons, one who helped to make her famous and added lustre to her name.

The world has lost one of its great benefactors.

In the heart of the flower and in the beauty and sweetness of the world he has perpetuated himself.

And in the starry firmament of immortality is seen a new star—and there appears this illustrious son of America—this great and good man—this Scientist, Naturalist, Humanitarian and Infidel—Luther Burbank.

THE BIBLE AND
THE PUBLIC SCHOOLS

by

Joseph Lewis

Author of "The Tyranny of God," "The Bible Unmasked,"
"Lincoln, the Freethinker," "Burbank, the Infidel," "Jefferson, the Freethinker," "Atheism," "Franklin, the Freethinker," "Voltaire, the Incomparable Infidel," "Shall Children Receive Religious Instruction?" "Mexico and the Church," "Spain: Land Blighted by Religion," etc.

THE FREETHOUGHT PRESS ASSOCIATION, INC.

317 EAST 34th STREET, NEW YORK, N. Y.

PUBLISHERS' FOREWORD

On May 25, 1930, Mr. Joseph Lewis as taxpayer, and on behalf of the Freethinkers of America, of which he is President, instituted legal proceedings to take the Bible out of the Public Schools of New York.

The case was argued before Justice John Ford of the Supreme Court of the State of New York, First Department.

Mr. Arthur Garfield Hays presented the arguments to the court on behalf of Mr. Lewis, and Mr. W. E. Mayer represented the Corporation Counsel of the City of New York.

On June 24, 1930, Mr. Justice Ford dismissed the complaint "without opinion." An appeal was taken to the Appellate Division of the Supreme Court, First Department, and on June 9, 1931 the same attorneys presented their arguments for their respective clients.

On July 9, 1931, the Appellate Divsion, consisting of Justices Finch, Merrell, McAvoy, Martin and Sherman approved the decision of Justice Ford, "without opinion."

An appeal from their decision has been taken to the Court of Appeals of the State of New York.

The question of the Bible in the Public Schools, up to that time was left entirely in the hands of the respective attorneys to be fought out upon purely legal grounds.

However, on July 23, Mr. Charles H. Tuttle, former Federal District Attorney for the Southern District of New York, and late candidate for Governor of the State of New York, and now President of the Greater New York Interfaith Committee, whose purpose it is to put religion into the Public Schools, spoke before the Rotary Club of New York, at their weekly luncheon at the Hotel Commodore, and viciously attacked both Mr. Lewis and the Society he represents, as "fanatical secularists" for their endeavors to take the Bible out of the Public Schools of New York.

Importuned by numerous friends to defend himself and the cause he represented, Mr. Lewis wrote the following letter:

July 24, 1931.

Secretary, Rotary Club of New York,
Hotel Commodore, New York City.

Dear Sir: I note in this morning's paper, that Mr. Charles H. Tuttle delivered an address before your organization yesterday. That Mr. Tuttle is suffering from religious hallucinations goes without saying. But when a former district attorney, and a former candidate for the Governorship of New York State tells you that we are a fanatical sect because we are trying to uphold the fundamental American principle of the separation of Church and State, I think you owe it to us as a duty, to accord us the same privilege that you extended to him to present our side of this important public controversy.

We shall be pleased to furnish a speaker to present our point of view on any date suitable to you, or, if you wish, we would be very pleased to debate the question with Mr. Tuttle or anyone else.

Confident that you will see the justice of our request, and awaiting you kind reply, I am,

Very truly yours,

JOSEPH LEWIS.

In response to this letter, Mr. Lewis received a telephone call from Mr. Edwin H. Rushmore, Secretary of the Rotary Club of New York, inviting him to speak on the subject of "The Bible and the Public Schools," and present the Freethinkers' point of view of this important subject.

Acknowledgment of this invitation was incorporated in the following letter:

July 30, 1931.

Mr. Joseph Lewis, President
Freethinkers of America
New York City

My dear Mr. Lewis:

In accordance with our conversation of this morning we are looking forward to having you as our speaker on Thursday, August 6, 1931, at 12:30 o'clock, at luncheon at the Hotel Commodore, on the subject "The Bible and the Public Schools."

I am enclosing our weekly bulletins of July 21 and 28, announcing the luncheon at which Mr. Tuttle spoke, and giving a brief account of the meeting.

Very truly yours,

Edwin H. Rushmore, Secretary.

Mr. Lewis' address follows:

He who decides a case, though he may decide rightly, if he has not heard both sides of the question, has not done justice.

Fair play is only too glibly mentioned today without being practised; and tolerance is more observed in the breach than in the performance.

And so when an occasion presents itself where both of these cherished ideals become a reality, our thanks and appreciation are due—and I want the Rotary Club of New York to know how much I appreciate the opportunity they have given me to present our side of the important controversy of "The Bible and the Public Schools."

And if there are men in this audience, who, for the first time, are looking upon a Freethinker I want to assure them that I have no horns in the back of my head; that I have never been arrested for beating my child, or for deserting my wife, and I even pay my income tax!

I also want at the very beginning of my talk to assure you that anything I might say this afternoon should not be taken as a reflection upon the personal beliefs of anyone in this audience.

I would not deliberately hurt the feelings of a single individual, and although I would like to explain in detail our philosophy, I shall do my utmost to confine myself strictly to the subject of the afternoon.

However, you have invited me to present the Freethinker's point of view on "The Bible and the Public Schools" and it would be hypocritical on my part if I did not speak the truth as I know it.

We are opposed to the reading and teaching of the Bible in the public schools from both a legal and moral point of view; and although the legal phases of the case are in the hands of our attorneys, I think we, as laymen, can well appreciate the fundamentals upon which we base our case.

The Constitution of the State of New York, Section 3, Article 1, provides as follows:

> "Religious liberty: The free exercise and enjoyment of religious profession and worship, *without discrimination or preference*, shall forever be allowed in this state to *all* mankind."

When George Washington Butler, that eminent mountaineer representative to the legislature of the State of Tennessee, the gentleman who introduced the notorious antievolution bill, made the startling discovery, during the now famous Scopes trial, that God in his infinite wisdom did not write the Bible in the English of the King James' version, he was terribly perturbed.

If anyone attempted to use some other version of the Bible he would have considered it blasphemous.

He found out however, to his amazement, that there were not only other versions of the Bible but that no two were alike.

The Catholic version differed from the Protestant version and both in turn differed from the Hebrew version.

In view of these facts how can any one particular version or in fact all three versions be read in the public school, with children of every conceivable religious heritage, without violating both the spirit and the letter of the provision of the Constitution that I quoted.

Section 4, Article 10, of the Constitution of the State of New York says:

> "Neither the state nor any subdivision thereof shall use its property or credit, or any public money, or authorize or permit either to be used directly or indirectly, in aid or maintenance of any school or institution of learning wholly or in part under the control or direction of any religious denomination, or in which any denominational tenet or doctrine is taught."

Can anyone deny that the reading of the Bible, without note or comment, is in effect a denominational tenet and religious exercise?

Can anyone deny that the Bible is a religious book and that its purchase by public money is illegal and a clear violation of this article of the Constitution?

There is a provision in the charter of the City of New York which says that the Bible may be read without note or comment, but specifically mentions that the Board of Education shall NOT be competent to decide which version shall be read!

Perhaps the great brain of Mr. Tuttle will be able to solve this conundrum.

When the wise founders of this Republic incorporated in the Federal Constitution those provisions known as the Bill of Rights they did so with the full knowledge and understanding of their importance.

And what was the very first of those amendments? It said that, "Congress shall make no law respecting the establishment of religion or prohibiting the free exercise thereof."

Thomas Jefferson was responsible for the Bill of Rights, and if Mr. Tuttle is in this audience, I trust he will include the name of Jefferson among the "fanatical secularists" that he so eloquently characterized at this meeting two weeks ago.

> "When a religion is good, I conceive it will support itself, and when it does not support itself, and God does not take care to support it, so that its professors are obliged to call upon the civil authorities, 'tis a sign, I apprehend, of its being a bad one."

I want also to make sure that Mr. Tuttle includes Benjamin Franklin, whose words I have just quoted, in his category of fanatical secularists.

The late Chief Justice of the Supreme Court of the United States, William Howard Taft, said ". . . religion itself may not be taught in the public schools, or under associations so near to the public schools that they become part of the instruction."

And Ulysses S. Grant, said, "let us resolve that not one dollar of public money shall be appropriated to the support of any sectarian school. Keep the Church and State separate."

Include these two Presidents in your list, Mr. Tuttle!

But if Mr. Tuttle insists that his remarks were particularly directed at our organization, then he will have to include in his list of fanatical secularists such men as Rupert Hughes and Clarence Darrow, Sir Arthur Keith and Bertrand Russell, Dr. Henry Smith Williams and Dr. Philip G. Peabody, Ex-Premier Herriot of France and Thomas A. Edison.

And in response to an inquiry from me asking his opinion of Bible reading and Bible teaching in the public schools, Mr. Edison wrote:

> "I do not believe that any type of religion should ever be allowed to be introduced into the Public Schools of the United States."

Mr. Tuttle must also include the late Luther Burbank, whose noble character and invaluable contributions to humanity are only too well known.

If these illustrious men who are members of our organization, are fanatical secularists, then I want to tell you gentlemen that I am proud to be President of that organization.

When Dr. A. S. Draper was Commissioner of Education of this state he laid down this rule: ". . . Religious exercises of any character cannot lawfully be conducted in the public schools. Reading of the Bible or repeating the Lord's Prayer is a religious exercise."

The laws governing the public schools of this state specifically mention the subjects in which the child is to be instructed, and Mr. Tuttle knows, and the churches know, that religion is not one of them.

Bible reading in the public schools is religious instruction. It is a violation of the law.

Are the strenuous efforts of the Greater New York Interfaith Committee and their attorney Mr. Tuttle to inject religion into the public schools an admission on their part that they are unable to make the people adhere voluntarily to their creeds?

Must they have the machinery of the state to assist them in their endeavors to make adherents and supporters of their churches?

Is it possible that the people are too enlightened to support as truth dogma that has long since been proven to be founded upon superstition and mythology?

Must the public school system be used to bolster up the dwindling congregations of the churches?

And when the churches insist that the machinery of the government do the work that they are supposed to do, then is it not a public acknowledgment of their failure?

They want the government to do what they themselves are unable to accomplish. And why?

Because education has left the church lagging miserably behind. The churches insist that an adulterated product is better than a pure one.

We do not.

We believe that education makes for morality and that religion adulterates it with superstition.

When Mr. Tuttle tells you that the Bible in the Public School will cure crime, he is suffering from religious hallucinations.

If religion could cure crime we would today be living in a paradise.

If what Mr. Tuttle says is true, then the Middle Ages should have been the most moral in the history of Man.

Were they?

Read any authentic history and it will tell you that never in the history of the people of this earth did there exist a more demoralized or more licentious people.

Only a little more than a week ago, there appeared in the New York Press, (New York Times, Herald-Tribune, July 27, 1931) the report of Dr. Adelaide T. Case, Professor of Education at Columbia University. In this report of her examination of 1,000 pupils, she expresses her astonishment at "the surprising amount of prejudice and ignorance about religion" among the majority of these children.

She continues: "How can there be any religious tolerance and true understanding when youngsters of nine and ten have such bitter and intolerant ideas of other religions? Not only do we find a marked misunderstanding between Jew and Christian, but between Catholic and Protestant children as well."

Her reason, she says: "Too often the fault lies with the parents. It is in their power to mold and color all a child's beliefs."

It has been our contention for years that the instilling of religious beliefs in the minds of young and immature children intensifies the hatred and bigotry that must inevitably follow such teachings.

And I am glad to see our educators verifying our contention by a scientific analysis of this important phase of child education.

The prejudiced and preconceived notions that children receive from their parents regarding the religion of others is only renewed and stimulated with Bible reading.

If you send your children to school with hatred in their

hearts for other children of different religious belief, how can you expect peace and harmony in the world?

The parent who instills religious prejudice in the mind of his child not only poisons his mentality with the virus of an implacable hatred, but is guilty of a moral crime for which there is no expiation.

Let us begin right. Let us send our children to school with a tolerant attitude towards other children, and with a desire to seek the truth no matter where it leads. If we do that, we can be fairly confident that before long the dawn of brotherhood will break upon the earth.

Let me control the education of our public school children for one generation and I will perform an educational miracle.

I will not subtract a single item from the education that they now receive, but I will eradicate racial and religious prejudice and hatred from their hearts.

Perhaps the most important and significant educational test in recent years, was detailed in a paper read before the Ninth International Congress of Psychology, held at Yale University on September 6, 1929, when Professor Pleasant R. Hightower of Butler University, Indianapolis, Indiana, made the startling report of an examination of more than 3,300 children. The New York Times reported his address with this caption:

"STUDENTS OF BIBLE FOUND LESS HONEST"

Professor Hightower said:

> "People have been saying for years that if you give children a knowledge of the Bible they will walk the straight and narrow way. The results show that they will NOT walk the straight and narrow way. It does indicate very definitely that mere knowledge of the Bible of itself is not sufficient to insure the proper character attitudes."

A child must be taught the morality we wish him to follow. In facing the facts of life there is no magic wand by which we can accomplish what we desire. We must work and labor for what we want. We must be trained to perform our labors. It is a slow and painful process. Anyone who has taught children knows how difficult it is. And if any of you gentlemen present do not know how difficult it is to teach, just remember the task you had the first time you tried to teach your friend how to play golf, or your wife how to drive a car.

If we could teach children morality by merely reading a passage from the Bible every day, then every child would be a moral genius.

No, my friends, the teaching of morality is a far more difficult task than most people realize.

Give us knowledge, and a sense of understanding, and a high order of morality cannot help but follow.

Not very long ago this city was stirred by the exploits of a young desperado. I am referring to "two-gun" Crowley. The memory of his capture is still too vivid in our imagination to need repeating here. He boldly confessed the murder of an officer of the law. I want to cite his case to show you the difference between religion and morality.

If you tell me that what he was taught is not the religion that you would teach, then I must ask who is to determine the religion that is to be taught, and when I raise that question there comes to my mind the whole history of religious antagonism and wars; with their massacres and butcheries that have stained this earth with innocent blood for the past 2,000 years.

After Crowley's capture and his incarceration he was approached by the district attorney. He said: "Of course I killed that cop, I don't like cops. No, I don't want any lawyer. Get it over with. Repent? Hell, no! My conscience was never so clear in my life. What I want is a square meal."

The kind-hearted district attorney suggested a thick beefsteak. "No, sir; no meat for me," said the young killer. "Don't you know this is Friday?"

What did Crowley's religion teach him: that it was a greater sin to eat meat on Friday than to murder a man?

When Earle Peacox was apprehended after the frightful murder of his wife he was found to be the proud possessor of a medal for six years of perfect attendance at Sunday School.

And recently a man of the Jewish faith was arrested for some infraction of the law. He refused to eat any but kosher food while in jail! He was not going to take any chances to arouse the wrath of Jehovah.

These are but three of the hundreds of instances that are happening daily to prove that religion and morality are not the same.

And I have in my hand a letter received some time ago from Mr. Lewis E. Lawes, Warden of Sing Sing Prison. It is in answer to a letter of mine asking for the religious beliefs of the inmates electrocuted during the past ten years.

To me this is a very significant letter.

And unless we are ready and willing to face the facts we would not be fair to ourselves nor to the important subject under discussion.

Mr. Lawes' figures for those executed in Sing Sing for ten years are as follows: Catholics, 65.1%, Protestants, 26.6%, Hebrews, 6.1%, Pagans, 2%, Irreligious, 0.3%.

If what Mr. Tuttle tells you about religion and crime were true, the reverse of these figures would prevail. Not only are these figures true of Sing Sing Prison, but they are substantially the same in every country, almost without exception.

This condition proves that the more intense the religious instruction, the less is the sense of moral responsibility!

Professor Westermarck, in his monumental work, "The Origin and Development of Moral Ideas" (Vol. 2. P. 736) says "it has been noticed that a high degree of religious devotion is frequently accompanied by a great laxity of morals." Of the Bedouins, he found that with one or two exceptions, "the practise of religion may be taken as a sure index of low morality in a tribe."

And in quoting an authority of the Mohammedan people, he records that "those Moslems who attended to their prayers most regularly were the greatest scoundrels."

Among two hundred Italian murderers, Ferri did not find one that was irreligious; and Naples, which has the worst record of any European city for crimes against the person, is also the most religious city in Europe.

On the other hand, according to Havelock Ellis, "it seems extremely rare to find intelligent irreligious men in prison."

And Laing, the historian, who was anything but a skeptic, observed that there was no country in Europe where there was so much morality and so little religion as in Switzerland.

So, when Mr. Tuttle tells you that religion is the cure-all

of crime, he makes that statement either designedly, deliberately and maliciously, knowing it to be false, or he makes it through ignorance.

If the former, it disqualifies him as an honest representative, and if the latter, it precludes him from speaking with authority upon this important subject.

Does Mr. Tuttle think for a moment that if religion, as he wants it taught, would cure crime, that we would be opposed to it?

On the contrary, we would welcome it with open arms.

What Mr. Tuttle and the Greater New York Interfaith Committee propose has been tried and has failed. That is why we are so much opposed to it. His method has been discredited. We want a better and more efficacious system.

But I do not think that Mr. Tuttle or the members of the Greater New York Interfaith Committee are seriously interested in the question of crime. It is religion that they are so much concerned about.

Another question that is sometimes raised while discussing the Bible in the schools, is that we do not object to the reading of Shakespeare.

Why should we?

Is Shakespeare imposed upon the children by law as of divine revelation? Is Shakespeare read in the schools without note or comment?

On the contrary, Shakespeare is read and discussed and studied for the good that can be gotten from him, for the knowledge that can be gained from the study of the greatest literary mind that ever lived upon this earth. And when the Bible is put into our educational institution to be studied as Shakespeare is now studied, no one will be better pleased than we are. Because we advocate the study of the Bible. We advocate that it be studied with the same searching inquiry as any other book.

We do not for one moment want to convey the impression that our efforts to take the Bible out of the public schools is an attempt to interfere with the rights that parents possess to instruct their children in religion if they so desire.

If parents wish to instruct their children in a religious doctrine there is plenty of time outside of school hours and on Saturdays and Sundays for this purpose. To ask the public schools to do the work that properly belongs upon the shoulders of the parents and the churches is not only an unjust imposition but reveals a shameful shirking of their duty.

And it is a peculiar situation that those who are trying to uphold the law and the Constitution are put on the defensive by being called "intolerant" and "fanatical," while the churches and their paid representatives, who are deliberately making every effort to violate the law to attain their ends, are put in the light of the injured party.

The attitude of the churches in trying to break into the public schools and break down the safeguards which were so wisely provided in the Constitution reminds me of a man who, after robbing a store, runs down the street shouting "stop, thief," for the purpose of distracting the attention of the people from his crime.

How can the churches plead respect for law, when they are doing their utmost to violate it for their own selfish purposes?

They are merely trying to bootleg religion into the public schools, and bootlegging is obnoxious even if done by a churchman.

There is an old principle of justice, that if you come into a court of equity you must come with clean hands.

The injection of religion into the public schools breeds prejudice and hatred among the pupils. It intensifies their religious convictions, and discord and dissension must inevitably follow.

The fight to take the Bible out of the Public School and stop the singing of hymns is a movement that has been going on for decades. It is an endeavor to keep our public institutions free of religious influences, as well as to keep up with the march of intellectual progress.

The Bible cannot legally be read or taught in the State of Ohio. It cannot legally be read or taught in the States of Wisconsin, California, Illinois, Kentucky, Kansas or Washington.

And the last state to my knowledge where a decision has been secured on this question comes from the far western State of South Dakota. It was rendered by the highest court of that state in June, 1929.

After reviewing fully the question, the court said:

> "A review of the history and a comparison of our institutions with those of other nations where religion is under state control, reveals the wisdom of our policy. It will not do, by an ill-advised decision, to impair the liberty of conscience so carefully safeguarded in this country."

The charge is made that without the reading of the Bible our public schools are Godless.

The same court had this to say in answer to that:

> "Another premise to be firmly fixed is that the reading of the Bible, or the offering of prayer, or both, in opening the exercises, is devotional, and not a part of the secular work of the school. One serious complaint made by religious people is that by excluding such exercises we thereby make our schools Godless. Such complaints argue that the converse would be true if such exercises were allowed, indicating that such exercises are considered devotional."

I do not think that the members of the highest court of the State of South Dakota are "fanatical secularists," but I want to take the opportunity of congratulating them on their sound Americanism.

Secularism, gentlemen—the separation of Church and State—is the magic principle that has made this country the most outstanding success among the governments of the world.

When the time comes when such a system of government no longer exists in this country, the time will come when religious freedom will cease.

The reading of the Bible and the injection of religion into the public schools is the entering wedge that will eventually destroy this principle.

And the old adage is still true that "a little leak will sink a big ship" . . .

Would Mr. Tuttle and the misguided members of the Interfaith Committee have us surrender this principle?

Can an intelligent person, looking back upon the history of those governments which sanctioned religion in their public institutions, and reviewing the fearful destruction wrought by a connection of Church and State, want to see such a blight fall upon this Republic?

The public schools of this state provide for the secular education of our children; the teaching of those fundamentals which we all agree upon as the basis of truth and knowledge. They must be kept free from sectarian influences, influences which are diametrically opposed to all the principles of education and learning.

I have the utmost confidence in the efficacy of our public school system. Its work has been most commendable; its future of great potentiality. I hold that the public schools are the most fundamental and most important institution of America. It is indeed the "melting pot," and we do not intend to sit idly by while over-zealous religious forces seek to "season" it to their liking.

We send our children to the public schools, not to be made Protestants, Catholics, or Jews, but American citizens, and to be instructed in the fundamentals of education. They are sent to the public schools to be taught that each and every one is equal before the law, and that each possesses the inalienable rights of life, liberty and the pursuit of happiness.

And that man is an enemy to this country, an enemy to its ideals and institutions who seeks to corrupt that system with religion.

The record of the public schools needs no defense. They are a shining light to America and her principles of equality. Nowhere in the world has education better shown itself than in the splendid men and women who are the products of the public school system of this country.

For that reason we are opposed to the reading and the teaching of the Bible in the Public Schools.

We are opposed to the Bible in the Public Schools because we want to eradicate religious prejudice, bigotry and hatred. We are opposed to the Bible in the Public Schools because we want our children to receive the finest secular education that the world has to offer.

We are opposed to the Bible in the Public Schools because we want our boys and girls to grow up to be intellectually free and morally courageous men and women.

We are opposed to the Bible in the Public Schools because we want the future citizens of this country to be Americans in the best sense of that word.

Shall Children Receive Religious Instruction?

A DEBATE BETWEEN

Rev. Walter M. Howlett

Secretary of the Department of Religious Education
of the Greater New York Federation of Churches

and

Joseph Lewis

President, Freethinkers of America

Author of "The Tyranny of God," "The Bible Unmasked,"
"Lincoln, the Freethinker," "Burbank, the Infidel," "Jefferson, the Freethinker," "Atheism," "Franklin, the Freethinker," "Voltaire, the Incomparable Infidel," "The Bible and the Public Schools," "Mexico and the Church," "Spain: Land Blighted by Religion," etc.

THE FREETHOUGHT PRESS ASSOCIATION, INC.

317 EAST 34th STREET, NEW YORK, N. Y.

CONTENTS

COPYRIGHT, 1933

THE FREETHOUGHT PRESS ASSOCIATION, INC.

1st Large Printing, 1933
2nd Large Printing, 1938

SHALL CHILDREN RECEIVE
RELIGIOUS INSTRUCTION

A debate between Rev. Walter M. Howlett (Secretary of the Department of Religious Education of the Greater New York Federation of Churches) for the affirmative; and Mr. Joseph Lewis (President of the Freethinkers of America) for the negative.

INTRODUCTION

During the last week of September, 1932, The Greater New York Federation of Churches had carried on a program emphasizing and advocating the value of religion in education. Newspapers had given wide publicity to this "Religious Instruction Week."

Mr. Edward L. Wertheim, who represented The Greater New York Federation of Churches, conceived the idea that the efforts of his organization during "Religious Instruction Week" could be brought to a climactic finish by a public debate on that subject. He, therefore, secured the services of Reverend Walter M. Howlett and Mr. Joseph Lewis as the two men most eminently capable of advancing the arguments for and against religious education for children.

Through the courtesy of Mr. S. Theodore Granick, director of the "Forum Hour" on Radio Station WOR, it was arranged that the debate was to be delivered over that station on Sunday, October 2nd, 1932. Each speaker was permitted a presentation of fourteen minutes, and a rebuttal of three minutes.

The result of the debate, Mr. Granick explained, would be determined by the radio audience itself which would be invited to express its decision by vote, to be announced one week later over Station WOR.

PRESENTATION OF THE AFFIRMATIVE

RESOLVED: That Children Should Be Given Religious Instruction.

REV. WALTER M. HOWLETT
Secretary of the Department of Religious Education
of the Greater New York Federation of Churches

It is a self-evident fact that children should be given instruction. It would not be possible to conceive of an intelligent mind that would question such a statement. Education we must have—the only question to be discussed then this afternoon, as I understand it, is—

In its simplest form religious instruction has to do with our relationships with one another and our relationships with God. Religious instruction therefore would be instruction concerning the relationships between persons and between persons and God. Christian education, which is the religious education with which I am most familiar, would deal with what Jesus taught should be the relationships of persons and His conception of what the best relationship ought to be between persons and God.

Education has been defined as life. To put it in the schoolman's phrase—it is the continual reconstruction of experience. The great objective of religious education is the enrichment of life. Our Master said: "I came that they may have life, and may have it abundantly."—John x, 10.

The objectives of religious education have been defined under seven heads by the representatives of the Protestant denominations of the United States of America. Since they are the consensus of opinion of the great body of educators representing millions of people, these objectives are much more important than anything I could say independently. Therefore, let us consider them.

First, religious instruction seeks to bring the individual into a consciousness of God as a reality in human existence and a source of personal relationship to Him.

Let me be concrete. A child watches a beautiful sunset. His heart and his emotions are stirred within him. He is led to wonder and into thanksgiving that such beauty exists. When a parent turns these emotions of his child toward God as the Giver and Creator of this beauty that is religious instruction. Further when the little child, just learning to speak, kneels in prayer with the parents—or more often with the mother alone—and is taught in simple words to thank God for the gifts of life, for its beauty and its truth, and to ask God to help him take the right course and to obtain the victory in right living—that is for the child religious instruction in its most beautiful and most effective form. He begins to know God in his own experience. This experience will ever grow and widen as the child becomes older. Dealing with the scientific side of this, James' "Varieties of Religious

Experience" is one of the greatest books ever written and thoroughly scholarly.

The second great objective in Christian religious education is to experience God through the teachings of Jesus Christ. It is to experience Christ as Saviour and Lord and to accept and act on the assumption of Jesus that persons are of infinite worth.

The idea of God has evolved throughout the ages. Truth does not come to man full-blown but yields its meaning bit by bit—so man's idea of God. In the early ages this idea was crude. Jesus however reveals a God Who is a loving Father, Who cares for each individual person. In its simplest form, Jesus brought to the world the idea of the Fatherhood of God and the Brotherhood of man.

The third objective of religious education is character building.

Now it might be said that the teaching of morality produces character and it does to a certain extent. To make morality effective however there must be emotion. Someone has said that religion is morality tinged with emotion. Psychology has taught us that emotion is the power house to character building. Undirected power is dangerous. Religious instruction seeks to guide that power into the *right channels*. It recognizes that character building is progressive. There is one ideal for the little child, another for the growing child, another for the youth and another for age. *Character building is never completed—it is a growing process.*

Christian instruction seeks to lead the individual into an enthusiastic and intelligent participation in the building of a community and a world.

Character does not develop in a vacuum. It develops in relationships of people. It has to do with the building of a good community. America has examples enough of the anti-social character. To be concrete, it feeds the hungry. It seeks to cast out disease, ignorance, *prejudice* and war— that is religious education.

Religious education seeks to develop in growing persons the ability and disposition to participate in the work of the organized Church.

I am not dealing with any theory of the origin of the church. I am only saying that religious instruction is not confined to the home alone. It seeks to get together in the community in an organized way, which way is through the church or synagogue. One object is to worship God but the greater object is that righteousness and right relationships may prevail among men.

Sixth: Religious education seeks to develop in growing persons a particular theory of life and the universe.

Right living produces right thoughts and right theories. At the same time, right theories produce right living. It seeks to lead persons into a sound theory of the universe.

Seventh: One of the greatest teachers of the Christian religion said: "Whatsoever things are TRUE, whatsoever things are HONORABLE, whatsoever things are JUST, whatsoever things are PURE, whatsoever things are LOVELY, whatsoever things are of GOOD REPORT; if there be any VIRTUE, and if there be any PRAISE, think of these things."—Phil. iv, 8.

It leads children to appreciate the great literature of the world especially the Bible because it contains so much of what is most worthwhile. Then it leads to an appreciation of the lives of great men and women who have meant the most in bringing about a better world. So many of the great paintings of the world deal with religion. How many paintings of the MADONNA AND CHILD have we among the masterpieces of the world? Would you deny children the study of these? How many of the great paintings have to do with the heart of religious instruction? How much of the poetry, how much of the great prose, how much of the great architecture, how much of the music, of all art is based on religion! In fact, unless children are given religious instruction, the best that life has to give will be missed.

All the world without exception will agree that children should be given religious instruction in the widest sense of the term. The only question among intelligent men can be what is religious instruction—what should be included in it and what should be excluded? After all that is about all that our discussion this afternoon can deal with.

President Hoover gave an address on Thursday and referred to the Children's Charter and he has done what every other president has done from the beginning of time in this country—he has said that the morality and welfare of our people and in turn the well-being of our state, country and institutions depends upon religion. He made the aims of the

Children's Charter his own. He said: "For every child spiritual and moral training to help him stand firm under the pressure of life."

It is one thing to stand firm under the pressure of life—character we must have—it is another to have life and have it abundantly and this is the fruit of religious education.

PRESENTATION OF THE NEGATIVE

RESOLVED: That Children Shall Not Receive Religious Education.

By JOSEPH LEWIS
President, Freethinkers of America

This is not a question as to whether a parent has the *right* to instruct his child in religious matters.

The Freethinkers of America maintain that parents possess *not only a fundamental right* in this respect, but that it is the duty of society to see that *this right* is always respected and maintained. But however emphatic we are in stating the principle of the parent's inalienable right to instruct his child in religious matters, we are *equally as emphatic* in contending that the inculcation of religious doctrines into the mind of a child is not only philosophically wrong, but morally and ethically harmful and detrimental.

The right to do a thing, and the propriety of doing that thing, are two altogether different propositions.

Many parents claim the right to beat their children.

They maintain that without corporal punishment they are unable to "make them good."

We consider the beating of a child to be brutally cruel and morally reprehensible.

But many parents still accept the Biblical injunction, the substance of which is, to spare the rod and spoil the child.

Not only have parents claimed the right to beat their children, but corporal punishment, until recently, was inflicted upon children even in our own public schools.

As the beating of children has been found to be wrong both in principle as well as in practice, we no longer permit the teacher in our public schools to inflict physical punishment.

And we no longer permit our public institutions to give religious instruction to children. Why?

Because the entire fabric of religious instruction has been found to be both educationally useless and intellectually harmful.

And just as we have made definite progress in convincing parents that it is wrong to beat their children, so I trust it will not be long before parents are convinced of the detrimental effects of giving religious instruction to their children.

In discussing this question one must speak plainly and frankly if one is to be honest in his presentation. And the more serious the question the more important it is that the facts be presented as they are.

At the outset let me define what is meant by religion. Religion is that which deals with man's relationship to a god, and all the ceremonies attendant upon that belief. It consists in praying, in making sacrifices, in observing feast and fast days, and in the worship and fear of a god. To give any other definition of religion is to confuse the issue in an attempt to avoid its implications.

Religious instruction consists in inculcating into the mind of the child the doctrine of a particular dogma.

Of what that dogma consists does not concern us in this particular discussion. *It matters not which one it is.* The mere fact that it is based upon a presumed infallible revelation *is sufficient* to exclude it from the mind of a child.

All religious systems and all religions are fundamentally based upon the fear of a god.

And the religious tenet that "the fear of the Lord is the beginning of wisdom" is contrary to every principle of enlightened education.

Nothing has proved more harmful and detrimental to the building of character than the inculcation of fear into the mind of a child. We cannot expect children, who are saturated with fear, to grow up to be intellectually free and morally courageous men and women. Any instruction that carries with it a fear reaction should be avoided as a plague. Because the courage to face the facts of life is without question the most important and most essential element in child training and education. What the world needs today is not cringing, frightened minds, but bold and courageous ones.

No better advice in this respect can be given than these words of Thomas Jefferson. He said: "Fix Reason firmly in her seat, and call to her tribunal every fact, every opinion.

Question with boldness even the existence of God; because if there be one, He must approve the homage of reason rather than that of blindfolded fear."

Ethics deals with principles of conduct between me and my fellow-man, and morality is a code of rules by which the individual conducts himself. The more we know, the more intelligent we are, the higher are our principles of ethics and the more scrupulous are our morals. It is our contention that education makes for morality and religion adulterates it with superstition. There is no problem of human conduct, either in the field of ethics or in the realm of morality, that cannot be solved without the element of religion.

In fact, no human problem can be solved satisfactorily until religion has been absolutely and completely separated from it. Whenever man has sought to solve his problems in conjunction with religion his tasks have become more complicated, and his conclusions have proved disastrous.

No better proof can be given of this than the principle underlying our own government. Secularism—the separation of Church and State—is the magic principle that has made this country the most outstanding success among the nations of the world. And what has proved beneficial and successful in the social sphere will be more definitely beneficial when practiced by the individual.

Religion belongs in the field of speculative philosophy. And I challenge any one to disprove the statement that there exists today a single system of religion that has for its basis anything *other* than speculation. What an injustice it is, then, to impose upon the mind of a child speculative philosophy when the most acute adult minds are baffled by it.

The child has task enough in understanding the simple things of life, without complicating its mentality with propositions impossible of solution. To burden the child's mind with anything but the truth is to handicap its whole mental machinery.

Intellectual freedom is the birthright of every child. He who robs a child of that right commits, in my opinion, an unpardonable crime.

If we are at all concerned with the education of our children it becomes of paramount importance that the child be taught the truth. And no doctrine should be taught as fundamental that has not been subjected to the closest and most searching inquiry. And it is because religions are based upon faith, and not upon proven and indisputable facts, that we have so many diverse and conflicting systems.

And although many religious systems accept the same basis for their creeds, their differences as to interpretation have caused the most vicious and antagonistic conflicts; conflicts that have led to murder and massacres, and to the bloodiest wars man has ever suffered upon this earth. It is because of these wide differences of opinion regarding the interpretation of religion that its inculcation into the mind of a child becomes so pernicious.

It is just as easy to teach a child the truth as it is to teach it a falsehood. It is just as easy to teach a child the facts of life—the basic and fundamental principles of existence—as it is to fill its mind with weird superstitions and phantasies.

Teaching facts, and the truths of life, has the added virtue in addition to its being the truth. It possesses the rare quality of honesty. And I would rather be honest in teaching my child the facts and truths of life than in maintaining an institution, regardless of how sacred it may be held.

Mental honesty is, above all the attributes, the greatest virtue of the mind.

Cultivate in our children this virtue and nine-tenths of the problems of misconduct will be solved.

It is the contention of some parents that it is better to teach their children "some kind of a religion" with the hope and expectation that when the child becomes an adult it will then be able to determine for itself whether the religious instruction it received was true or false, and whether it should be retained or rejected.

If the harm of such instruction was merely its stupidity, then there would be no need for its condemnation. But the leaders of organized institutions of religion know that that which is impressed upon the mind of a child before the age of seven, molds and shapes the child's character. Only by the most heroic mental effort are men and women able to eradicate the teachings they received in childhood, but which are no longer tenable in the face of present day knowledge.

To inculcate religious dogma into the mind of a child, with the hope that when it grows older it will discover its falsity, is to perpetrate upon that child irreparable harm.

What would we think of a teacher who taught a child the

wrong principles of grammar, and gave as her excuse that when the child grew up, it would then be able to distinguish between the wrong instruction and the right principles.

What would we think of a teacher who taught a child that the way to arrive at a sum of figures is to multiply and subtract, hoping that in later life the child would discover the mistake, correct the false method, and free its mind from these entangling conclusions.

Giving a child religious instruction about matters that are based upon faith and belief, and of which there are no known facts, with the hope that the child in later life will discover the truth and free its mind of these confusing ideas, is just as stupid as it would be to inculcate the wrong principles of grammar and arithmetic.

Does any one think for a moment that if religious instruction to children were conducive to good morality that we would be opposed to it? On the contrary, we would most heartily favor it. It is because religious instruction has been tried and found wanting that we are opposed to it.

If children, given religious instruction, were more moral and offered better examples of proper conduct than those children whose education consisted solely of ethical instruction and moral precepts, then there would be no question about its benefits. But the facts are on the other side.

The most careful analysis and the most searching inquiry reveal that the children whose education is free from religious bias and influence, and who are taught strictly the rules of morality, are more upright and are often better examples of right conduct than those who received religious instruction.

Perhaps the most important and significant educational test in recent years was detailed in a paper read before the Ninth International Congress of Psychology, held at Yale University on September 6th, 1929, when Professor P. R. Hightower of Butler University, made the startling report of an examination of more than 3,300 children. The New York Times reported his address with this caption:

Students of Bible Found Less Honest

Professor Hightower said: "People have been saying for years that if you give children a knowledge of the Bible they will walk the straight and narrow way. The results show that they will NOT walk the straight and narrow way. It does indicate very definitely that mere knowledge of the Bible of itself is not sufficient to insure the proper character attitudes."

If we could teach children morality by merely reading a passage from the Bible every day then every child would be a moral genius. But the teaching of morality is a far more difficult task than most people realize.

Give us knowledge, and a sense of understanding, and a high order of morality cannot help but follow.

Recently I received from Mr. Lewis E. Lawes, Warden of Sing Sing Prison, a letter giving me the religious beliefs of the inmates electrocuted in Sing Sing during the past ten years.

And unless we are ready and willing to face the facts we would not be fair to ourselves nor to the important subject under discussion. Mr. Lawes' figures for those executed in Sing Sing for ten years are as follows: Catholics, 65.1%; Protestants, 26.6%; Hebrews, 6.0%; Pagans, 2.0%; Irreligious, 0.3%.

If religious instruction were conducive to a high degree of morality, then the reverse of these figures would prevail. And not only are these figures true of the State of New York, but they are substantially the same in every state, almost without exception.

This condition *proves* that the more *intense* the religious instruction the *less* is the sense of moral responsibility!

Only a little more than a year ago, there appeared in the New York press, the report of Dr. Adelaide T. Case, Professor of Education at Columbia University. In this report of her examination of over 1,000 pupils, she expresses her astonishment at "the surprising amount of prejudice" among the majority of these children.

She continues: "How can there be any religious tolerance and true understanding when youngsters of nine and ten have such bitter and intolerant ideas of other religions? Not only do we find a marked misunderstanding between Jew and Christian, but between Catholic and Protestant children as well."

The reason, she says: "Too often the fault lies with the parents. It is in their power to mold and color all a child's beliefs."

It has been been our contention for years that the instilling of religious beliefs in the minds of young and immature children intensifies the hatred and bigotry that must inevitably follow such teachings.

And I am glad to see our educators verifying our contention by a scientific analysis of this important phase of child education.

The prejudiced and preconceived notions that children receive from their parents, regarding the religion of others, is only renewed and stimulated with religious instruction.

If you send your children into the world with hatred in their hearts for other children of different religious belief, how can you expect peace and harmony in the world?

The parent who instills religious prejudice into the mind of his child not only poisons that child's mentality with the virus of an implacable hatred, but is guilty of a moral crime for which there is no expiation.

Let us begin right. Let us keep our children free from religious prejudice. Let us send our children out into the world with a tolerant attitude towards other children, and with a desire to seek the truth no matter where it leads. If we do that, we can be fairly confident that, before long, the dawn of brotherhood will break upon the earth.

REBUTTAL BY THE AFFIRMATIVE

REV. WALTER M. HOWLETT

Mr. Lewis is talking about an age long since gone. He is a very learned man but in regard to religious education, its objects and what it seeks to do, he is no more an authority than I would be on atheism. The basic idea of religious education is not fear but love, love of God and love of fellow man. "Thou shalt love the Lord thy God with all thy heart, and with all thy soul, and with all thy mind. This is the first and great commandment. And the second is like unto it, Thou shalt love they neighbor as thyself. On these two commandments hang all the law and the prophets." These are the words of Jesus. I will leave it to any intelligent person to decide if these teachings are dangerous to children. Are children likely to be better or worse if they are taught to base their lives in such practices?

Mr. Lewis says that the teaching of religion means the teaching of falsehood. The Master said: "Know the truth and the truth shall make you free." All modern and up-to-date religious education is based on this idea, whether it be Christian religious education or otherwise. The open mind, the search for truth, the testing of things, is basic in religious education. Is an attitude of this kind likely to better social life?

Then he fears that in view of the fact that there are different religions, that because I have dealt with Protestant Christian religion, I have brought in a dangerous principle. Does he know that all religious education, no matter what the division may be, teaches pupils to seek the truth and that great religious movements are co-operating? Witness in this respect our Interfaith Committee in New York City where the three great faiths co-operate in the interests of childhood of our city and the welfare of our country.

Again he says criminals label themselves Protestant, Catholic or Jew, and only 0.3% label themselves Pagan or irreligious. It is true that practically all people do label themselves as belonging to some faith or other. There is not even 0.1% of our people in America who would not label themselves under one or another. Thus the so-called Pagans or irreligious, even according to the figures Mr. Lewis gives, have many times their normal percent of criminals according to their quota of the population. Is he aware that scientific investigation has shown that those who really practice religious living, speaking generally, do not commit crimes?

Then Mr. Lewis quotes Dr. Adelaide Case and Professor P. R. Hightower. He fails, however, to get the point in each of these instances. I am well acquainted with this great teacher, Dr. Adelaide Case, and familiar with her work. If any reader will study the book and the article quoted he will find that what each is contending for, is a particular method in religious education. What they really say is that religious education to be effective must be "learning by doing," not by memorizing Bible verses in general or abstract principles about virtue. People do not become virtuous in that way, they acquire virtue and righteous living by "being and doing." It is only thus that religious education is effective.

No intelligent person teaches falsehoods or hate, or the beating of children for that matter. Teaching religious education is summed up in "What doth the Lord require of thee, but to do justly, love mercy and to walk humbly with thy God." Teach children to practice this kind of living and life will be more satisfying; their future will be sure and our country will be a better place in which to live.

REBUTTAL BY THE NEGATIVE

Joseph Lewis

"To make morality effective there must be emotion," says Rev. Mr. Howlett.

The most dangerous person in the community is the man or woman obsessed with religious emotion. Our insane asylums are filled with religious maniacs. The man who shot President Doumer of France was deeply religious. He said that he committed his crime by the direction of God. The assassinator of President Garfield said in his defense that God told him to commit his dastardly crime. The daily papers are filled with crimes committed by the homicidal religiously insane.

Instead of its being an argument in favor of religious instruction, morality mixed with religious emotion is one of the most pertinent reasons why children should NOT receive religious instruction.

No child should be taught to pray to God for help, not only because the prayer will not be answered, but because it is a selfish act. The height of selfishness is to ask for something you have not worked for. And to teach a child to pray has still an additional objection. It undermines the *strength of will* which is so necessary to character building.

This illustration is pertinent.

Two little girls were on their way to school. As they approached the school house, the bell rang, which meant that they should be inside the building. One little girl, brought up in a religious home, said to the other: "O, Mary, we are late, let us pray." The other little girl, the daughter of Freethinkers, hastily replied: "O, NO. Let us RUN."

I challenge the statement of Rev. Howlett that religious instruction teaches a child to appreciate the lives of the great benefactors of the human race. Invariably our great men have been martyrs to the cause of truth. Galileo was imprisoned; Bruno and John Huss were burnt at the stake by the religionists of their time. In our own day we see Thomas Paine, the author-hero of the American Revolution denied his proper place in American history because of his irreligious opinions. And when Thomas A. Edison died, a teacher of religion had the brazen effrontery to berate the American people for honoring so great a man merely because he rejected the religious opinions of his day.

Religious instruction narrows a child's mentality to the scope of the particular religious dogma it receives. The teaching of ethics and morality, *free* from religious bias, permits a child to weigh the opinions and thoughts of the world.

Some of the points raised by Rev. Mr. Howlett injected sectarianism into this debate, and that is what I wanted to avoid.

I wanted to discuss this question purely from a philosophical and educational point of view. To discuss it from the angle of sectarianism would only add another argument against giving children religious instruction, because it would provoke antagonism from many sides.

The test made by Dr. Case, which I mentioned in my presentation, proves the harm of the very instruction proposed by Rev. Mr. Howlett. It is sectarianism that has caused man's inhumanity to man, and you cannot separate sectarianism from religious instruction.

We want our children to be instructed in the highest principles of ethics and the soundest code of morals. This cannot be done as long as they are associated with religious dogma. Not until we keep our children free from religious bigotry and prejudice will the human race make any definite progress towards peace and understanding.

RESULT OF THE VOTE ON THE DEBATE BY THE RADIO AUDIENCE

> As previously explained in the Introduction, the winner of the debate between Rev. Walter M. Howlett and Mr. Joseph Lewis was determined by the recorded votes of the radio audience.

On Sunday, October 9th, 1932, Mr. S. Theodore Granick announced over Radio Station WOR that the public vote on the question "Should Children Receive Religious Instruction" stood more than three to one in favor of Mr. Joseph Lewis, who had spoken against it.

MEXICO AND THE CATHOLIC CHURCH

by

Joseph Lewis

Author of "The Tyranny of God," "The Bible Unmasked,"
"Lincoln, the Freethinker," "Burbank, the Infidel," "Jefferson, the Freethinker," "Atheism," "Franklin, the Freethinker," "Voltaire, the Incomparable Infidel," "The Bible and the Public Schools," "Shall Children Receive Religious Instruction?" "Spain: Land Blighted by Religion," etc.

THE FREETHOUGHT PRESS ASSOCIATION, INC.

317 EAST 34th STREET, NEW YORK, N. Y.

EDITORIAL FOREWORD

IT IS common knowledge that, ever since the successful establishment of the Republic of Mexico during the administrations of Presidents Obregon, Calles, and Cardenas, there has been a terrific conflict between the Government and the Roman Catholic Church.

The crisis has been severe. Blood has been spilled in actual insurrection by the Church and its followers.

If for no other reason, the religious crisis in Mexico has held the nationwide attention of our country. It was, therefore, decided that a public debate be held on the subject so that the question could be presented by men who were competent to discuss the question, and who could be considered representative of the opposing forces.

Through the courtesy of Mr. S. Theodore Granik, the facilities of the "Forum Hour" on Radio Station WOR, on Sunday, July 7, 1935, were offered.

The subject selected for the debate was:

"Is Mexico's Religious Policy Justified?"

The affirmative was supported by Mr. Joseph Lewis, President of the Freethinkers of America.

The negative was taken by Hon. William J. Boylan, Member of the House of Representatives of the United States from the State of New York.

The publishers must offer an apology to readers of this pamphlet. In printing a debate it is but common courtesy to publish the addresses of *both* speakers. Unfortunately, in this instance, Congressman Boylan declined to permit the inclusion of his address.

Yet, even though Congressman Boylan's address is missing, it is felt that those who read Mr. Lewis's presentation as contained here will be satisfied that they have obtained every fundamental point of the subject—especially since the public vote, as received by the officials of WOR, stood nearly two to one in favor of Mr. Lewis.

Radio Address Delivered by Mr. Joseph Lewis,
President of the Freethinkers of America,
Over Radio Station WOR Sunday,
July 7, 1935, on the Question:

"IS MEXICO'S RELIGIOUS POLICY JUSTIFIED?"

I CONSIDER it a great privilege to defend the Mexican people in their present religious controversy with the Catholic Church.

From the facts in my possession, coupled with indisputable records from the pages of history, not only do I justify the Mexican people in curbing the activities of the church, I also believe the firm stand they have taken was necessary to their security and peace.

In debating an important question of this kind it would be an act of cowardice on my part if I failed to speak the truth which the facts demand.

Where human liberty and human life are involved, I do not consider any institution too sacred to be exposed. Nor do I believe that the ends of justice can be achieved by remaining silent upon a subject, merely because a religious institution is involved.

No wrong can be too old or too venerable to be attacked.

And he who decides a case, though he may decide

rightly, if he has not heard both sides of the question has not done justice.

In my opinion, there is no question of religious liberty involved in this controversy.

If this were a question of religious freedom, I would plead with all the power and strength that I possess not only for the Catholic Church, but for any church; and not only for any church, but for any individual.

I do not believe that religious liberty depends upon arguments.

It is a fundamental human right.

Although I believe that religion has been a retarding influence upon the intellectual and social life of the human race I would not, for a single moment, deprive any person of the right to worship or to hold any religious opinion he desires.

This right, however, belongs equally to the person who does not worship and who is free from any religious beliefs whatsoever.

But religion, to an even greater degree than charity, covers a multitude of sins.

When a religious organization aligns itself with the forces of reaction it cannot cry "Intolerance" and "Persecution" if it meets the forces of progress.

Catholicism is not the native religion of the Mexican.

It is foreign and alien to his nature.

It was not until the year 1521, that an emissary of the Pope planted his flag upon Mexican soil.

Shortly thereafter, the simple faith of the Aztecs was destroyed.

All of their sacred literature and religious symbols were consumed in flames, and the population baptised en masse into Catholic Christianity.

From that day began the exploitation of a people, almost unparalleled in history.

In addition to being robbed of their possessions, they were forced to adopt this alien religion at the point of the sword.

So abject did they become that not only their lands, but even their domestic animals, had to be blessed by the Church—for pay.

And on November 4, 1571, there was established in Mexico, under the dominant rule of the Catholic Church, the most hateful institution that ever existed upon this earth,—The Inquisition.

The palace of the Inquisition in Mexico City is now the National School of Medicine.

On April 11, 1649, one hundred and twenty seven persons were burned to death for violating the laws prohibiting religious liberty.

The Mexican people in their fight against tyranny, corruption and exploitation, found that it was first necessary to break the strangle-hold that the Catholic Church had upon their lives.

No government could exist in Mexico, until the present successful revolution, which offered the slightest semblance of freedom and equality to its people as long as the Catholic Church possessed the resources, controlled the education, and dictated the policies of the nation.

Four hundred years of uninterrupted rule gave the

Catholic Church absolute dominance over fifteen million Mexicans.

No word of mine, no argument that I could advance, could as pertinently tell the story of this dominance and its degradation as the facts of history itself.

The progress of a nation is determined by the welfare of its people.

What did these four hundred years of absolute domination by the Catholic Church do for the Mexican people?

What was their condition before the revolution of 1857?

It was one of subjection and abject poverty.

What was their average in education? It was one of the lowest on the American continent. 85% were illiterate.

What was their standard of living?

Hardly better than that of slaves.

What was their per capita wealth?

The Church either owned or controlled nearly 90% of this immensely valuable land.

No country in the world had become so pauperized through the avarice of the church. It became known as the "paradise of religious orders."

What was their political situation?

They were vassals of the Church.

Did they possess religious freedom?

How could they? The laws under which they lived for over three hundred years expressly prescribed the Roman Catholic religion, and proscribed all others.

The first Mexican constitution, adopted in 1824, under

the domination of the Catholic Church, specifically provided that "The religion of the Mexican nation is and shall perpetually be Roman Catholic—and forbids the exercise of any other."

This is not the first time that the Catholic Church has maintained that the Mexican people have been unfriendly to it.

When the constitution of 1857 was formed, Pope Pius IX denounced it in scathing terms and pronounced the anathema of the Church upon it.

When General Plutarco Elias Calles was President and sought to enforce the reformed constitution of 1917, based upon the Constitution of 1857, not only were there loud cries of "persecution", but an edict of excommunication was threatened against the people.

And what happened?

The Government of Mexico insisted upon the observance of its laws.

And what was the result?

In 1926 the present Pope placed an interdict upon the people, and the Catholic Church in its entirety went on strike.

For three years it refused to participate in the religious exercises of the Mexican people.

And it was my prediction then, and I think subsequent events have verified it, that those three years proved to be three years of momentous importance in the intellectual and political life of the Republic.

During this period the Mexican government laid the substantial foundation for a new social order, bringing to the enslaved Mexican people the first ray of light of political and social freedom that has brightened their dark horizon during more than four centuries.

While the three-year strike of the Catholic Church lasted, other religious organizations continued to function, and when services were resumed, the hierarchy discovered that it had lost thousands of its communicants.

Laws satisfactory to other religions should certainly be good enough for Catholicism.

Mexicans are not the only people who have found it necessary during the past centuries to curb the power of the Catholic Church.

France, Italy, Spain, Germany and England found it necessary, for the stability of their government and for the welfare of their people not only to curb, but in some instances to expel the church.

The pages of history speak for themselves.

The religiously deluded youth who assassinated President-elect Alvaro Obregon wore under his shirt, over his heart, a picture of the Virgin of Guadalupe when he committed this dastardly deed.

Today, a Mother Superior is serving a sentence of life imprisonment for her participation in this crime. In a solemn religious ceremony she blessed the pistol that fired the fatal shot.

Evidence raises the suspicion that the Catholic Church supported the reprehensible and traitorous Huerta in his campaign of conspiracy against the Mexican people, which ended in the assassination of their beloved President— Francisco Madero.

Even if the clergy had nothing to do with the murder of Madero directly, they rejoiced at his death.

For two days following his burial, services of celebration were held in their churches throughout the land.

What would our government do if a church persistently violated our laws, flouted our efforts to establish a system of secular education, and was suspiciously associated with the assassination of our presidents?

I think the attitude of the Mexican people in this crisis is one of great restraint and lenity.

It is only when the Catholic Church becomes an instrument of political intrigue that the Mexican people insist that its priests be silenced, and its subversive activities halted.

If an individual is known to be an habitual criminal greater precautions are used to protect society from him.

A defiant, meddling, domineering and conspiring religious institution can easily become Public Enemy Number 1.

Thomas Jefferson must have had Mexico in mind when he said:

"In every country and in every age the priest has been hostile to liberty, he is always in alliance with the despot, abetting his abuses in return for protection to his own."

Mexico is now living under a constitution which compares very favorably with, and in some respects, is admirably in advance of our own.

The Mexican constitution, like our own, provides for

the secular education of its children, and for the rights of conscience in matters of religious belief.

We cannot object to another country's flattering us by its imitation of our laws, especially if those laws are the fundamental basis of *our* government.

Our constitution says:

"That Congress shall make no law respecting the establishment of religion or prohibiting the free exercise thereof."

And the present Mexican constitution, concerning the same subject, reads:

"That Congress shall not enact any law establishing or forbidding any religion whatsoever."

It is these provisions of the Mexican constitution to which the Catholic Church takes exception.

It wants to repudiate this constitution for the one which provides for the existence of the "Roman Catholic Apostolic Religion as the national religion, without toleration of any other."

It also wants the statutes revived providing for the "Benefit of Clergy."

But the Mexican people, like the peoples in other enlightened countries, insist that the temporal power of the church shall no longer prevail in their country, and they insist that the church confine its activities and functions solely and exclusively to matters of a religious nature.

The church as a divine institution belongs to the same category as the belief in the flatness of the earth.

The days of theocracies are over. Religion cannot dictate to free governments.

Neither individuals nor religious institutions can complain of the laws under which they live if, because of their persistent violation of those laws, freedom is denied to them.

With a well organized and well oiled machinery of propaganda the religious problem in various countries could be stimulated and magnified to such menacing proportions that it would embroil the entire world in one of those bitter and devastating religious wars which have stained the pages of history with blood.

Religious intrigue has, on more than one occasion, precipitated bloodshed, and unless we are willing to take heed of the past it will do so again.

Almost every government in the world has had its religious problem, and if the United States were to interfere in each and every one of these countries every time a religious dispute arose, our country would be meddling with the internal affairs of almost every nation on the face of the globe.

We ourselves are not without our racial and religious problems.

Let us make sure that our house is in order before we seek to arrange the affairs of others.

The American people believe that the religious situation in Mexico is purely a problem which concerns them and them alone, and it is our intention to let them solve it.

Secretary of State Cordell Hull has just issued an official

communication in which he states that the government of the United States does not intend to interfere with the religious affairs of Mexico.

He gives as his reason for this action that not a single complaint has been received by him from an American living in Mexico, whose religious liberty has been abridged in the slightest degree.

The enlightened people of the United States want to live in peace and harmony with the rest of the peoples of the world, and with no greater degree of good will does this apply than to the people of our sister republic below the Rio Grande.

Courts of equity were formed for the purpose of administering justice, but one of the cardinal principles of these courts is that those who seek redress shall come to them with clean hands.

Can the Catholic Church in Mexico do that?

Has it been free from the crimes which it now charges Mexico with perpetrating against her?

It is a matter of historical record that the Mexican people have been far more liberal with the Church than the Church has been with them.

The present political leaders of Mexico are men of the highest ideals who have dedicated themselves to the cause of freedom, and I am confident that future generations will honor General Calles, President Cardenas, and other Mexican leaders, with the same devotion that we honor George Washington and the Revolutionary Fathers.

To enjoy the fruits of a Revolution is quite a different

thing from enduring the suffering and hardship of living through one.

I cannot conclude this defense of the Mexican people in their present religious controversy more appropriately, than by firmly and emphatically stating that there is a greater degree of religious liberty in Mexico today than there was at any time during the four hundred years of its domination by the Catholic Church.

GEMS FROM INGERSOLL

By Joseph Lewis

Address delivered over Radio Station WGBS,
New York City, May 26, 1926

Robert G. Ingersoll was not only America's greatest
writer and orator, but he was also one of the grandest men
who ever lived. He was not only a soldier, but also a
patriot. He was a poet as well as a philosopher, a benefactor and a humanitarian.

He was in the fullest, broadest sense a man among men,
a genius among intellectual giants, a mountain standing
amidst the hills.

Just before his death, Luther Burbank said in a letter
to Ingersoll's oldest daughter, Mrs. Eva Ingersoll Brown,
"His life and work have been an inspiration to the whole
earth, shedding light in the dark places which so sadly
needed light."

It was Luther Burbank, if you remember, who re-
quested that Ingersoll's eloquent oration to his brother
be read at his burial.

And Mark Twain said of Ingersoll:—

> He was a great and beautiful spirit; he was a
> man—all man—from his crown to his foot soles.
> My reverence for him was deep and genuine. I
> prized his affection for me, and I returned it with
> usury.

And I hold in my hand a letter from humanity's greatest benefactor, who has written me his appreciation of Ingersoll especially to be read to you tonight. He says:—

> I think that Ingersoll had all the attributes of a perfect man, and, in my opinion, no finer personality ever existed. Judging from the past, I cannot help thinking that the intention of the Supreme Intelligence that rules the world is to ultimately make such a type of man universal.

The writer of this letter is Thomas A. Edison.

But perhaps the best description of Ingersoll comes from a member of his family. An admiring friend once said to his youngest daughter, Mrs. Maude Ingersoll Probasco, "Your father was a great man," and she impulsively exclaimed: "My father was not a man, he was a god."

It is generally said, however, that Ingersoll was a destructionist, that his philosophy was of a negative character; that he tore down and did not build up.

Never was a grosser misrepresentation ever made of a man and his labor. Only those who are not acquainted with Ingersoll and his works; only those who do not understand his purpose; only those who are ignorant or prejudiced about what he sought to accomplish could make such a statement. For no man had a deeper regard for humanity; no man loved humanity more fervently; no man did more to bring understanding and peace to humanity than this infidel, this unbeliever.

He labored to abolish war, and fought to establish an international court to settle disputes between nations. He said, "Every good man, every good woman, should try to do away with war, to stop the appeal to savage force."

Throughout history, the man who has been ahead of

his time, the leader, the pioneer, has always been misunderstood, vilified, maligned, and slandered.

The man who has defied convention and proposed new methods for the world to follow has always suffered at the hands of those who did not understand him.

The fighter for human rights and liberty who pays the penalty for his daring, who is heaped with calumny and vilification and branded with the epithet of heretic, infidel, and blasphemer in his own days, is generally remembered by future generations with magnificent monuments in loving memory of his unselfish labors on behalf of mankind.

Ingersoll himself has said, "The infidels of one age are the aureoled saints of the next."

And as it was with Hypatia, Bruno, Servetus, Galileo, Spinoza, Thomas Paine, and Lincoln, so it is with Ingersoll.

Robert G. Ingersoll was a destructionist in the same sense that Columbus was when he destroyed the belief in the flatness of the earth. He was a destroyer in the same sense as the fathers of this Republic were when they destroyed a despotic monarchical government. He was a destroyer in the same sense that Lincoln was when the great emancipator destroyed the abhorrent institution of slavery.

"The destroyer of weeds and thistles is a benefactor whether he soweth grain or not," said Ingersoll. And he did both.

He destroyed hatred and eradicated prejudice from the human mind. He helped to free the intellect from the superstition of a degrading religion and to emancipate the race from the tyranny of fear.

He also planted seeds; seeds which have taken root, and from which have grown precious fruit.

Here are but a few of the gems of Ingersoll. Let these few gems be an introduction to you to become more familiar with the writings of this man.

Contrary to what is known as Ingersoll's belief, the great Agnostic believed in heaven, and here is his description of it:—

> If upon this earth we ever have a glimpse of heaven, it is when we pass a home in winter at night, and through the window, the curtains aside, we see the family about the pleasant hearth; the old lady knitting, the cat playing with the yarn; the children wishing they had as many dolls or dollars or knives or somethings as there are sparks going out to join the roaring blast; the father reading and smoking, and the clouds rising like incense from the altar of domestic joy. I never passed such a house without feeling that I had received a benediction.

How much understanding, happiness, and joy has this gem brought to those of wedded life! And from what volume could better advice be given?

> It is not necessary to be great to be happy; it is not necessary to be rich to be just and generous and to have a heart filled with divine affection. No matter whether you are rich or poor, treat your wife as though she were a splendid flower, and she will fill your life with perfume and joy.
>
> And do you know, it is a splendid thing to think that the woman you really love will never grow old to you. Through the wrinkles of time, through the mask of years, if you really love her, you will always see the face you loved and won. And a woman who really loves a man does not see that he grows old; he is not decrepit to her; he does not tremble; he is not old; she always sees the same gallant gentleman who won her

hand and heart. I like to think that love is eternal. And to love in that way and then go down the hill of life together, and as you go down, hear, perhaps, the laughter of grandchildren, while the birds of joy and love sing once more in the leafless branches of the tree of age.

And this is what he said of love:—

Love is the only bow on life's dark cloud. It is the morning and evening star. It shines upon the babe and sheds its radiance on the quiet tomb. It is the mother of art, inspirer of poet, patriot, and philosophy. It is the air and light of every heart, builder of every home, kindler of every fire on every hearth. It was the first to dream of immortality. It fills the world with melody—for music is the voice of love.

Love is the magician, the enchanter, that changes worthless things to joy, and makes right royal kings and queens of common clay. It is the perfume of that wondrous flower, the heart, and without that sacred passion, that divine swoon, we are less than beasts; but with it, earth is heaven, and we are gods.

Ingersoll believed in the "Democracy of the home and the Republicanism of the fireside." He said that "men are oaks, women are vines and children are flowers," and how many men have been made more gentle, and women more tender and children holier by these words?

When your child commits a wrong, take it in your arms; let it feel your heart beat against its heart; let the child know that you really and truly and sincerely love it. Yet some Christians, good Christians, when a child commits a fault, drive it from the door and say: "Never do you darken this house again." Think of that! And then these same people will get down on their knees

and ask God to take care of the child they have
driven from home. I will never ask God to take
care of my children unless I am doing my level
best in that same direction.

Call me Atheist, call me infidel, call me what
you will, I intend so to treat my children, that
they can come to my grave and truthfully say:
"He who sleeps here never gave us a moment
of pain. From his lips, now dust, never came to
us an unkind word."

On one occasion, after delivering this excerpt in an
address in Washington, a United States Senator sought
him and said, "Colonel, you have converted me. For
years I have been estranged from my only daughter because she did not marry to please me, but now I shall go
to her tonight, and beg her forgiveness for allowing a
selfish pride to keep her from my arms and heart!"

And not even Shakespeare has surpassed in poetic
beauty and expression this gem:—

The laugh of a child will make the holiest day
more sacred still. Strike with hand of fire, O
weird musician, thy harp strung with Apollo's
golden hair; fill the vast cathedral aisles with
symphonies sweet and dim, deft touches of the
organ keys; blow, bugler, blow, until thy silver
notes do touch and kiss the moonlit waves, and
charm the lovers wandering 'mid the vine-clad
hills. But know, your sweetest strains are dis-
cords all, compared with childhood's happy laugh
—the laugh that fills the eyes with light and
every heart with joy. O rippling river of laughter, thou art the blessed boundary line between
the beasts and men; and every wayward wave of
thine doth drown some fretful fiend of care. O
Laughter, rose-lipped daughter of Joy, there are
dimples enough in thy cheeks to catch and hold
and glorify all the tears of grief.

Many have asked what did Ingersoll believe, did he have no creed? Oh, yes! he did, and this is the way he expressed it:—

THE CREED OF SCIENCE

To love justice, to long for the right, to love mercy, to pity the suffering, to assist the weak, to forget wrongs and remember benefits—to love the truth, to be sincere, to utter honest words, to love liberty, to wage relentless war against slavery in all its forms, to love wife and child and friend, to make a happy home, to love the beautiful in art, in nature, to cultivate the mind, to be familiar with the mighty thoughts that genius has expressed, the noble deeds of all the world, to cultivate courage and cheerfulness, to make others happy; to fill life with the splendour of generous acts, the warmth of loving words, to discard error, to destroy prejudice, to receive new truths with gladness, to cultivate hope, to see the calm beyond the storm, the dawn beyond the night, to do the best that can be done and then to be resigned—this is the religion of reason, the creed of science. This satisfies the heart and brain.

Like Shakespeare, it is doubtful whether there will ever live another man to possess Ingersoll's brilliancy of language. His expressions glitter like diamonds and pearls. But it will not be many years more before the heart of humanity will be indelibly impressed with the genius of "The Great Agnostic."